PN
4193   SIMMONS   47848
.I 5   New speakers handbook
S5

Illinois Central College
Learning Resources Center

NEW SPEAKERS HANDBOOK

*a professional speech writer's collection
of the best, wittiest and most
profound openings, closings, anecdotes,
witticisms and philosophical comments,
along with advice on how to use them
to give polished, memorable public talks
on all subjects and in all situations*

THE DIAL PRESS • NEW YORK • 1972

S. H. SIMMONS

NEW SPEAKERS HANDBOOK

How To Be the Life of the Podium

INTRODUCTION BY DAVID SUSSKIND

FOREWORD BY STEPHEN O. FRANKFURT

Excerpts from *Self-Renewal* (Harper & Row, 1964)
and from *Excellence: Can We Be Equal And Excellent Too?* (Harper & Row, 1961)
both by John W. Gardner are reprinted by permission of the publisher.

Library of Congress Cataloging in Publication Data

Simmons, Sylvia H.
  New speakers handbook: How to be the life of the
podium.

  1. Public speaking. 2. Quotations. I. Title.
PN4193.I5S5   808.5′1   72–4545

Printed in the United States of America
First Printing

For Hans, Steve, Eddie,
John, Harry, Vic, Martha, Frank,
George, Ed, Pete, Jim,
Dana, Jack, Dorothy, Andrew, Norm,
Wil, Louise, Bob, Marion,
Fran, Al, Amos, Kit, Bill, Les,
Carl, James, Greg,
Claire, Henry, Brad, Mac, Gene,
and all the others who
were courageous enough to pretest
this material for me
in their platform appearances

*I am deeply grateful to
Lawrence J. Muller
for his encouragement and
incisive editorial suggestions . . .
and to Cele Cicchetti
for her dedicated
and painstaking assistance
in readying this manuscript for
the printer*

TABLE OF CONTENTS

INTRODUCTION

After so many years of involvement with various forms of theater, I like to think that I know what excites an audience. And, obviously, Sylvia Simmons, the author of this book, knows, too. Unfortunately, there are an awful lot of public speakers who don't.

I've attended more conventions, symposia, seminars and public meetings than I care to remember and if I were to take all the speeches I've ever heard and lay them end to end, they would stretch from sheer hell to ho-hum and back again.

I'm really amazed that so many people who have reached the apex of success in their own fields have a tendency to turn to stone when faced with an audience of more than half a dozen people.

Even men and women who are great conversationalists tend to "lecture" when they get up on a platform.

They never think to use the very things that ordinarily make them good conversationalists—anecdotes, humor, quotations . . . any of the devices which can make a speech or a conversation come alive—and what comes out sounds like it was hacked out of dull concrete.

Obviously, the author of *New Speakers Handbook: How To Be the Life of the Podium* knows first hand what stirs an audience and causes it to react. Her experience with speakers and speeches is so practical and extensive that anyone faced with a platform appearance should find considerable help in this handbook of eminently usable and quotable material. What makes it valuable is that it's quality advice: up-to-date and right on target for today's audiences.

Whether you're going to talk to a convention hall full of business giants or to a handful of your fellow PTA members, I'd be surprised if this handbook didn't help you get cheers from your audience.

DAVID SUSSKIND

FOREWORD

When I was the president of Young & Rubicam, Inc., the second largest advertising agency in the world, I was often invited to appear as a guest speaker before business, civic, academic, and social groups. I was frequently an after-dinner or after-luncheon speaker, sometimes the keynote speaker on a program, and, occasionally, the recipient of some award or other that called for an appropriately dignified and humble "recipient's acknowledgment," as the programs are wont to list it.

Since my business commitments kept me going at the traditionally hectic pace of Madison Avenue, it was essential for me to have a "ghost," and I was fortunate enough to be able to swipe Sylvia Simmons from the Chairman of the Board and get her to write my talks; or, in those instances when I found the time to draft my own rough scripts, to get her as my speech doctor. Her fine pen and quick wit eventually touched every speech, except impromptu ones, that I ever gave and, thanks to her talents, I soon became a favorite of program chairmen from London to Tokyo.

As a matter of fact, even some of my impromptu talks have been enhanced by the material in this book. Half of Madison Avenue knew that Sylvia kept locked in her desk a voluminous file of index cards, each of which carried a single story or line that she or some of her equally accredited ghost friends had used with great results in the talk of some important personage to some equally important audience. She was constantly besieged by requests to borrow the file or, when she was willing and available, to "doctor" a dull script with material from her private collection. I was one of the few people privileged to have access to this file and, often faced with the need to talk on very short notice—to some audience of client brass (our clients ranged from the Chrysler Corporation and Union Carbide to General Foods and Procter & Gamble), or perhaps to some visiting delegation from abroad, or perhaps to a college class—I would rummage through Sylvia's material in the hope of finding some appropriate comments with which to enliven the more serious aspects of my message. She never failed me. I always found such a plethora of good stuff that I was sometimes tempted to throw away my script and just flip sophisticated lines at my audience, much as a stand-up comic might do. Fortunately, good sense (usually Sylvia's) prevailed.

However, over the years I grew more-than-passingly familiar with what became known as "Sylvia's File," and once, in London, it certainly saved the reputation I enjoyed as a raconteur. I had been invited to England to bring a message from the colonies to the London Television Advertising Congress, an audience that was a veritable Who's Who of British businessmen and their advertising agency counterparts. Many of my own agency's international clients were in the audience. The organizers of the Congress had chosen to employ a complicated audio-visual device. They had set up twelve "monitors"—small TV screens—along the sides of the huge auditorium so that members of the audience, wherever they sat, could get a close-up view of each speaker. Both sound and pictures were transmitted to television trucks (parked three blocks from the auditorium) and relayed back again to the monitors. I thought the idea silly; but then, I was only a foreign guest speaker.

In accordance with Parkinson's Law, which tells us that anything which can go wrong *will*, the equipment broke down, and there was no substitute equipment in the auditorium that could project the film—without which my talk was meaningless. To make matters worse (for me), I happened to be the speaker at the mike when all systems wouldn't go. Afraid that this high-powered audience might just get up and leave, the program chairman sent a cryptic note up to me. It said, "Just *talk!*" Well, what in the world can a man say under those circumstances—and for fifteen minutes that seemed like forever?

As a technician hung a temporary neck mike around my sweating collar, Sylvia's file flashed before my eyes and, without quite knowing where I was headed, I followed the chairman's instructions; I talked. "Let me use this waiting time," I said, "to tell you an old Russian fable that is not inapplicable to the situation in which our program chairman now finds himself." And then I told the Russian fable that appears on page 357 of this book. Immodest as it may sound, I must tell you that it brought the house down. Those dignified British executives howled and stamped their feet, and when they began to smack their water glasses with their pencils, I realized they wanted me to give them more. I culled my memory and, one after another, Sylvia's anecdotes and one-liners began to come to me. I can't say that I delivered them in very sensible sequence, but the audience had a great time during the fifteen-minute wait upon technology.

To this day, I still occasionally meet someone in London who will say, upon introduction, "By George, aren't you the chap who's so good on his feet?" Surely I could not have achieved such international fame as a wit and public speaker were it not for my extraordinary ghost-writer.

STEPHEN O. FRANKFURT

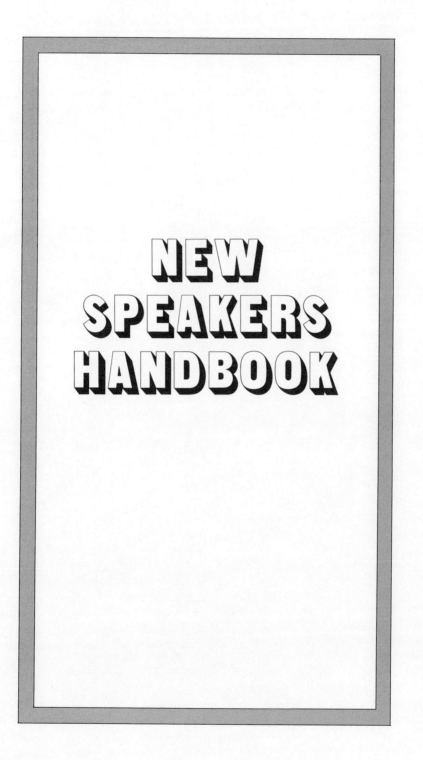

NEW SPEAKERS HANDBOOK

A FEW INSIDE TIPS
FROM THE AUTHOR

In *New Speakers Handbook*, I have drawn upon my twenty years of experience as a professional "ghost" to give you some inside tips of the trade, along with my heretofore private collection of openings, closings, jokes, anecdotes, and philosophical comments with which I have enhanced and enlivened many speeches—and, in so doing, earned more than half a million dollars during my career.

I must warn you that this handbook is not designed to tell you *how* to deliver a line, improve your phrasing, or use a microphone. For that, you need a coach or director. Few people, aware that their public performances are not all they would have them be, ever consider engaging the services of a local theatrical director to coach them before a scheduled performance. Yet I have found that, even in New York and London, quite famous stage direc-

3

tors (who are, perhaps, between plays) are willing, if the price is right, to "direct" a non-theatrical public speaker in advance of his platform appearance.

What this book *will* do for you is supply you with a choice of material that will help you get into your talk, enliven it along the way, and get off while the getting is good. And it will give you, briefly and in simple language, some practical advice about writing a talk that will get you the sort of applause every speaker wants.

I have, wherever possible, indicated where I first heard or read a given piece of material. That is not to say that, in every case, the source given is actually the first person ever to have said it. It is merely where I heard it. And since the contents of this book were collected over a period of some twenty years—during which time I ghost-wrote several hundred speeches for business ty-coons, politicians, doctors, publishers, and paid lecturers —many anecdotal sources have long since been forgotten. In some instances, the source of a line or passage is myself, since I have chosen to include lines of my own creation *where they have been tested in successful platform use.*

A few words of explanation about my use of the pronoun *I* in this handbook. In all the explanatory copy— wherever I tell how to write something, or where I de-scribe a technique or give advice on using this book or some specific material in it—the pronoun *I* refers to me, the author of this book. For example, in the previous paragraph of this section, when I said, "I have . . . in-dicated where I first heard or read a given piece of material," the first person pronoun refers to your author.

However, wherever I provide actual material for you

to use in preparing your talk—openings or closings, anecdotes, philosophical comments, witticisms, etc.—the
material, where appropriate, has been written in the first
person to make it easy for you to see how it might be used
in a speech. In all those instances, the pronoun *I* is meant
to be *you*—you the reader, the person talking to an audience.

Here's an example. In the chapter entitled "Openers," you will find this item suggested as a "throw-away"
line which a speaker can use while adjusting the microphone: "I'm always a little intimidated by a microphone.
Of course, a microphone never made a fool of anybody.
It only shows them up!" Should you decide to use that
comment in one of your own speeches, you could use it
exactly as is—because the first-person copy is written just
the way you would deliver the line from the platform.
This cuts down the amount of time you would otherwise
have to spend in editing suggested material for your own
personal use. In addition, all the items given in this book
have been selected because they have been successfully
platform-tested; they were written for the *ear,* and by
presenting them as an audience would hear them, you
can get a better idea of how they would actually sound in
platform use. (Only the chapter entitled "The Wisdom of
the East" contains some material I have not personally
tested. Keen interest in India and China is of such recent
vintage I have not had the opportunity to use all of those
items in speeches I've written. But I do stress the timeli-
ness of that material for today's public speaker.)

Let me give you another example. In the chapter on
Politics, you will find this opening to a short story: "One

of the young men in my office said to me the other day, 'You know, I have half a mind to go into politics.' " In this instance, the *me* means *you,* the reader, the user of this platform bit. If you used this particular anecdote, you would say those very words, "One of the young men in *my* office . . ." Of course, there could be other changes you might want to make. If, for instance, you are a teacher, you would change the line to say, "One of the young men in my *class* . . ." But the first person pronoun would remain—it's *you.*

Here's a word of practical advice concerning publicity and the special material you select for use in your talks: if you speak frequently, and especially if your talks are likely to be covered or reviewed by trade or local press, *don't* include your jokes and anecdotes in press release copies. This will enable you to use your best material over and over again as you grow comfortable with it and find from your own experience that it will work for you. This was an old trick of John F. Kennedy's, a master at using anecdotal material and one-liners. In place of the opening comments, your release copies should either carry the words "Introductory Remarks" or begin immediately with the first serious paragraph.

You will, occasionally, have people in the audience write to you for "a copy of that great fable you used at the end of your talk—which was not included in the script I wrote for, which you so graciously sent me . . ." You can then decide whether you want to succumb to the flattery and send the writer your fable—or whether you want to tell him to get his *own* ghost-writer.

Finally, there are two indices at the back of this book.

Each is more than just an index; each is a carefully designed aid to help you write and deliver a more memorable speech. I urge you to read "How to Use This Index" which prefaces each of those listings. These explanations will suggest new ways to approach the talk you're preparing so that your final presentation is varied, witty, and as enjoyable as those given by even the most gifted and sought-after platform personalities.

S. H. S.

OPENERS

getting into
your speech

It is very comforting and reassuring to get some form of response from the audience shortly after you have uttered your first words. Whether that response is laughter, applause, or even an invited groan, at least you know the sea of faces out there are not the dismembered heads of some hostile force, waiting for its first opportunity to snicker, sleep, or—God forbid!—snore. Only one thing can be worse than that: telling an opening story and having it lay an egg. The silence can be deafening.

Thus, the toughest job a speaker has is breaking the ice and developing some sort of rapport with the audience. Once that's done, most speakers will relax a bit. With relaxation comes better delivery and heightened audience attention. I do not advocate, however, that a speaker merely tell any old funny joke he knows in order to unwind or to hear the welcome sound of laughter.

Openers should track directly into the talk—by acknowledging the introduction about you that the chairman or moderator has just delivered; by explaining your presence on the program; by saying something regarding the audience or subject matter; or by letting the audience in on some aspect of your personality or state of mind. You will see how this works as you go through the "openers."

I have also included some material, dealing with the matter of writing or giving speeches, which can be inserted in a talk at the beginning, although sometimes at the end. Some of these are no more than attempts to woo the audience. Interestingly enough, audiences do not resent this. On the contrary, they set you up as being human or modest, or maybe just one of them. Anyone in your audience who has ever dealt with the problem of preparing a talk, or who would like to give one but feels inadequate to the task, will identify with you if you let him in on your own trepidations.

How do you know whether your opener is going to work? There is no guarantee. But there are a few things you can do to increase the odds. Every one of the openers given here *has* worked—for someone else. What you need to do is pick the one or two openers that you will feel comfortable with. Close the door and say them out loud —several times. If your choice gives you a chuckle and you're not ill at ease with the concept, consider using it. Then consider your audience. Break it down in your own mind. Who will be out front? Have you met any of them? Do they have the intellectual capacity to grasp the tag line? Are they likely to have enough humor to appreciate a story that kids them a bit? Are they your peers? If so, will they allow as how the story includes you, along with them, in the joshing?

When you've selected your opening, grow familiar with it. *This is very important.* Read it out loud ten times. Change the words that you stumble over and substitute words of your own choosing. Don't feel hemmed in by the particular phraseology given here. However, don't change any word or phrase essential to having the audience understand the punch line.

Try out the story, if it *is* a story, on someone in your family or at the office. Possibly, they won't like it. Don't be discouraged. Remember that your speech will be given in a big room, to a large number of people waiting for something clever or astute or informative to be said. The listener's mind-set will be quite different from that of the audience-of-one on whom you're practicing your material. The true purpose of such practice is for you to become accustomed to telling the story or saying the line, so that your eyes are not glued to the script page when you eventually deliver it from the platform. Use your practice situation to learn where you might improve audience understanding by using greater emphasis or by pausing at given points. While I do not recommend memorizing your talk, it will increase your self-confidence if you know your opening lines by heart.

And now, how about these for openers . . .

¶

Before I begin, I'd like to tell you the name of that main course you just had for lunch—in case they ask you when you get to the hospital.

¶

Thank you for that very complimentary introduction. Of course, I am not unaware that flattery is 90 per cent soap. And soap is 90 per cent lye.

¶

I deeply appreciate your very generous introduction. Even if I believed only 50 per cent of it, I would be flattered. I don't really think that flattery can hurt a man—unless he *inhales.*

¶

I have considerable respect for your tolerance in inviting me to address you—and for my courage in accepting.

¶

This is an appropriate story to tell when you've been called upon to give an impromptu talk. It can also be used for a prepared talk if a particularly large burst of applause greets the speaker.

Some years ago, the British House of Commons was interrupted by the news that the cable to Africa had been completed.

After the huzzahs and hat-tossing had died down, Winston Churchill rose to say, "Excellent, excellent. Now, what shall we *tell* the Africans?"

¶

The following is a fine story with which to open your talk if you are the last speaker on the program.

I cannot help thinking about the minister who gave the invocation at a church conference. "O Lord," he said, "give the first speaker the power to provide inspiration here today. And Lord, help the second speaker to convey the seriousness of his message to all assembled in this room. And Lord, have mercy on the last speaker."

¶

On the way in, I noticed an announcement on the bulletin board that some of you may have missed. It said that the meeting of the local Clairvoyance Society had been cancelled—due to unforeseen circumstances.

> Follow this up with some comment such as: "I do not consider myself clairvoyant, but I've accepted your challenge to discuss the future and so . . ."

¶

> If you are called upon to introduce another speaker, you might end your introduction by saying:

The relationship of the toastmaster to the speaker should be the same as that of the fan to the fan dancer.

It should call attention to the subject, but not make any particular effort to cover it. Ladies and gentlemen, I give you [name of speaker].

¶

> This comment can be used by a speaker who is called upon to give a talk at break-fast or at any early hour of the morning.

I hope I can manage to keep myself awake during this talk. Frankly, I'm unaccustomed to getting up so early in the morning. Until I got the invitation to appear in this spot, I didn't even know there were two eight o'clocks in the same day.

¶

I am, of course, pleased and flattered by your kind introduction. But then, I suspected all along that, someday, somebody would kick over the basket and unbushel my shining light.

¶

I feel a little like the son of an Arabian sheik who was having a birthday. His father didn't quite know what to give a boy who had everything, but he finally hit on the idea of giving him a harem. After presenting the gift, the sheik left his son alone.

Some time later, passing by, he noticed the boy standing befuddled outside the harem door. "What's the matter, son?" asked the sheik. "Don't you know what to do with it?"

"It's not quite that, father," replied the son, "It's just that I don't know where to start!"

> You might then go on to bridge from the story into your talk by saying that your subject is such a broad one, or has so many ramifications, that you almost "don't know where to start."

¶

> This is a throw-away line that can be used as you adjust the microphone to the proper height and direction.

I'm always a little intimidated by a microphone. Of course, a microphone never made a fool of anybody. It only shows 'em up!

¶

Let me assure you at the outset that I am not here to tell you how to run your business. There are far too many people meddling in your business already.

Life

¶

I am not going to cover everything I believe on this subject. First, it would take more time than I have allotted to me. Second, I am ever mindful of something that Joseph Addison once wrote in the year 1711.

"If the minds of men were laid open," wrote Mr. Addison, "we should see but little difference between that of the wise man and that of the fool. The great difference is that the first knows how to pick and cull his thoughts for conversation, by suppressing some and communicating others; whereas the other (the fool) lets them all indifferently fly out in words."

¶

If you wear glasses and have to put them on to read your script and take them off to see the audience, or if you wear bifocals, this story acknowledges the glasses at the onset so that you need not apolo-

gize later on for any "business" of
putting them on and taking them off.

I'm just getting used to these bifocals and I hope I can
manage to read this small type in my script. I know
that when I look over the top of them at some of our
cute young secretaries in the office, they probably
think, "That guy's a little bit eccentric." But I'd rather
have them think that than *not* wear the glasses, and
have them say, "That poor old sonovabitch is going
blind!"

¶

I hope I can remember the lines I am going to ad-lib.

This line works particularly well if you
make a thing of placing your script on the
podium in such a way that the audience
can see it is quite substantial. Or, if you
really want to play it for a laugh, bring an
extra copy of your talk to the podium with
you; drop it helter-skelter, so that the audience can see the pages fall all over the
platform; wait for them to gasp in sympa-
thy; then deliver the line and proceed
from there by reading your duplicate
paper.

¶

For use in introducing a speaker:

I couldn't possibly tell you all the impressive things
about him that could be told. In fact, his *Who's Who* is
more than seven inches long.

¶

In introducing another speaker with an
impressive list of accomplishments and
memberships, tick off his various associa-
tions and memberships, such as "Member of the Board of———," etc., then use
this line:

He is, in fact, so busy he couldn't make it here tonight.

¶

The subject you have asked me to address myself to
is such that I am reminded of a letter that a ladies'
club once wrote to Charles William Eliot when he was
president of Harvard. "Dear Mr. Eliot," they wrote.
"Our Club Committee, having heard that you are the
country's greatest thinker, would be greatly obliged if
you would send us your seven greatest thoughts."

The bridge between this opener and the body of the talk might go something like this: "I'm not going to burden you with my seven greatest thoughts. But I do have five [or seven, or ten] points I want to make here today concerning [subject of talk]."

¶

This is an appropriate opening when you are substituting for someone who had been scheduled to speak, but was unable to make it:

Mr. [name of scheduled speaker] sends his regrets and me . . . I mean, he regrets to send me . . . I mean, he sends me with his regrets.

¶

Once upon a time, in the days of the Roman Empire, a mob was gathered in the Coliseum to watch as a Christian was thrown to a hungry lion. The spectators cheered as the wild beast went after its prey. But the Christian quickly whispered something in the lion's ear and the beast backed away with obvious terror on his face. No amount of calling and foot stomping by the audience could get the lion to approach the Christian again. Fearlessly, the Christian walked from the arena.

The Emperor was so amazed at what had happened that he sent for the Christian and offered him his freedom if he would say what he had done to make the ferocious beast cower in fear. The Christian bowed before the Emperor and said, "I merely whispered in the lion's ear: 'After dinner, you'll be required to say a few words.'"

It is always flattering to receive an invitation to address an audience such as this as the after-dinner speaker. It is also somewhat unnerving to arrive at the moment of truth and wonder whether you have enough to say to keep a well-fed audience awake for another half hour.

¶

A man brought his mule to a mule trainer and said he was having a lot of difficulty with the animal. The trainer agreed to take him on and they started work immediately.

The trainer picked up a heavy club and smacked the mule in the rear end, causing the mule to fall down. It staggered to its feet, only to have the trainer hit it another resounding blow with the club. As the beast toppled again, the owner said, "Wait up! Hold on! I didn't bring that animal here to be clobbered. I brought it here to be trained. What kind of training is that?"

To which the trainer replied, "Oh, that's not part of the training. That's just to get his attention so that I can *start* to train him."

I confess that that story is not part of my talk. It's designed to get your attention so that I can start to make my pronouncements.

¶

That was a very gracious introduction, and I thank you for it. It reminds me of the time that a toastmaster delivered an equally flattering introduction when he was called upon to introduce Adlai Stevenson. He thought he had invoked virtually every compliment and bit of praise that he could without being fawning, so he was surprised when Mr. Stevenson got up and said, "Thank you very much, sir. That is probably the *second* most flattering introduction I have received."

This really bothered the toastmaster, because he felt he had gone about as far in his comments as anyone could have gone. But Mr. Stevenson, sensing his dismay, went on to say that there had once been an occasion when a toastmaster had been delayed and was unable to perform the introduction. Under those circumstances, Mr. Stevenson had had to introduce himself.

I have never had to introduce myself, so permit me to say that I have never had a more generous introduction.

¶

I am delighted that everyone here is in some way connected with the field of [title of subject].

Occasionally, I am called upon to address an audience that is as heterogeneous as a low-priced sausage. In those instances, finding the common denominator is not easy. Fortunately, I have no such problem today.

¶

As I stand before you, I can't help thinking about the man who was killed in the floods in Florence, Italy just a few short years ago.

He made his way to heaven, and at the Pearly Gates he was asked to give his case history—to tell the story of how he died and came to heaven. This he obligingly did. St. Peter thought the story so interesting that he asked the new arrival if he would agree to give a talk to the other angels in heaven, telling them all about the flood and his demise.

The newly arrived resident of heaven was very much flattered, and he immediately accepted the invitation. As he flew away, a kind young angel tugged at the sleeve of his robe and said, "Sir, I think I ought to tell you that *Noah* will be in the audience."

My point is that I'm somewhat abashed at being up here and talking on the subject of [fill in] when so many of you in the audience are experts in the field.

¶

Well, as Lewis Carroll wrote in *Through the Looking Glass*:

> *"The time has come" the Walrus said,*
> *"To talk of many things;*
> *Of shoes and ships and sealing-wax,*
> *Of cabbages and kings."*

I am not going to talk of shoes, ships or sealing-wax, but I do have on my list a number of subjects that include [list topics to be covered].

¶

That introduction credits me with just about every flattering thing in the book. About the only thing you left out was the Boy Scout's oath—I don't believe you mentioned that I am "trustworthy, loyal, helpful, friendly, courteous, kind, obedient, cheerful, thrifty, brave, clean and reverent."

Well, I want you to know I am all those things, too, although they have little bearing upon the subject of my talk, which is—as you know from your program —[name of talk].

¶

The art of persuasion can be stated in five words: Believing something and convincing others. Unfortunately, my talk will require more than five words. I didn't have time to write a *short* speech. But I hope that when I have finished, I will have persuaded you to share my point of view on the subject of [title of subject].

¶

William Makepeace Thackeray once said that "The two most engaging things a writer must do, are to make new things familiar—and familiar things new."

In writing this talk, I have concentrated on making some new things familiar to you. I hope that when I have finished, I will not only have familiarized you with these things, but convinced you of their merit.

¶

Before beginning my talk, I would like to give you Adlai Stevenson's rule for speech writing:

> *"If you would make a speech or write one*
> *Or get an artist to indite one,*
> *Think not because 'tis understood*
> *By men of sense, 'tis therefore good.*
> *Make it so clear and simply planned*
> *No blockhead can misunderstand."*

I know there are no blockheads in our audience today —but, in writing my talk, I have tried to keep things clear and simple. If in so doing I have oversimplified things, bear with me, for I have done so in the interest of clarity.

¶

There is an old speech writer's maxim that goes something like this:

> *First I tell 'em what I'm going to tell 'em.*
> *Then I tell 'em what I'm telling 'em.*
> *Then I tell 'em what I told 'em.*

Time does not permit me to follow that outline. So without any preamble—nor do I intend to make any summary in my conclusion—let me get to the heart of what I want to tell you.

¶

Johann Wolfgang Goethe, the German writer and poet, once made this statement regarding his own work: "The greatest genius will never be worth much if he pretends to draw exclusively from his own resources. What is genius but the faculty of seizing and turning to account everything that strikes us? Every one of my writings has been furnished me by a thousand different persons, a thousand different things . . ."

In what I am about to say, I lay no claim to originality.

¶

After-dinner speakers are almost always men. Women can't wait that long.

> If you are a woman speaker, you might then add a comment to the effect that you are, therefore, surprised to have been chosen as tonight's after-dinner speaker.

¶

Every successful speech has two parts. First, there must be a plan or a dream about what you want to say; the second part is the execution of that plan. Both parts are necessary in order to achieve success on the public platform. The hard thing about this is getting started on the execution.

Most people who have a good plan for a talk find themselves in a situation similar to that of the golfer who was teeing off his ball on a short hole. He told his golf partner, "I should be able to make this in one long drive and a putt." Then he got up and took a couple of practice swings before he let go at the ball. The ball rolled off the tee a distance of about twenty feet. The golf partner turned to the fellow who had such a splendid plan for his play on the hole and remarked dryly, "Now all you need is one hell of a putt."

Well, when I accepted this invitation, I had a helluva fantasy about what I was going to tell you. I hope that what I have jotted down here proves as interesting to you as the plan was to me.

¶

Mark Twain was a speaker at a meeting. He was brilliant and witty. After him, Chauncey De Pew was the next speaker. He was embarrassed to speak after the great Twain speech. He got up and said, "I want to thank Mark Twain for having given my speech."

> This is a nice way to acknowledge an excellent talk that preceded yours and to warn the audience not to expect as much from you as from the previous speaker.

¶

A visiting clergyman was to deliver a sermon at the campus church at Yale University. He announced that his sermon would be divided into four parts—each initialed, so to speak, by the four letters of the university's name. Starting out with Y, he talked about the God of the Jews, using His Hebraic name, Yahweh. Moving on to A, he talked about Amos, or maybe it was Aaron. In like manner, he found inspiration in the letters L and E.

After the service, two students who had heard the visiting clergyman talk were discussing what they had heard. "Quite ingenious," said one, "building his sermon around Y-A-L-E."

"It sure was," said the other, "but I'm glad I didn't hear him preach at the Massachusetts Institute of Technology."

I shall try to be brief up here today . . .

¶

I speak in public so often that many people often ask me if I have a ghost-writer. The fact is, I don't. I wouldn't dare let anyone write my speeches for me. Not since I heard the story of a very busy corporation executive who hired a speech writer.

The writer did an excellent job for many months and felt he was entitled to a raise. He approached his boss with his demands and was flatly turned down. No amount of persuading would get the tycoon to raise his salary.

Not long afterwards, he was called upon to write another speech, and he went to work on it. His boss didn't have time to look over the script before his scheduled appearance in public. Shortly before he was due to go on, he rushed into the writer's office, grabbed the manuscript, and ran for a taxi. He arrived at the luncheon just as he was about to be introduced.

He opened his script and, after reading some introductory remarks, began to castigate the audience for having failed to take positive action on an important industry issue.

"There is not one of you here in this room," he read, "who is to blame. *Everyone* here is to blame! Have you not sat back and suffered the status quo to continue? Have you not been content to rest on your profits while the industry atrophies from lack of intellectual nourishment? I tell you, we must take some constructive action. And I am going to suggest to you a ten-point program, without which this industry will never survive its competition. Here are my ten points."

With that sentence, the speaker reached the end of the paragraph and turned the page. The next page of his script was completely blank except for one sentence in the middle of the sheet. It read: "O. K., you cheapskate, from here on in you're on your own!"

And so, without benefit of ghost-writer, here goes with my own deathless prose . . .

¶

I'm going to read my talk to you today, rather than deliver it off the cuff. That's because I believe it's a good idea to think through my thoughts carefully before I say something. The trouble is that it never sounds any better than if I had just blurted it out in the first place.

¶

I will not pretend that the ideas I am about to set forth in this speech have all originated with me. I am a great borrower. I am, in fact, a little like Dale Carnegie, who wrote, in his famous book entitled *How To Win Friends and Influence People,* these words:

"The ideas I stand for are not mine. I borrowed them from Socrates. I swiped them from Chesterfield. I stole them from Jesus. And I put them in a book. If you don't like their rules, whose *would* you use?"

¶

I suppose I ought to explain how I came to be invited to appear as your luncheon speaker here today. What happened is this. [Name of program chairman] called me up and said, "Say! I want to ask you something. You believe in free speech, don't you?"

And I said, "Yes, naturally, of course I believe in free speech!"

So he said, "Great! Come on down and give one."

So here I am.

YOUR SPEECH WILL ALMOST WRITE ITSELF

if you follow
these easy steps

In most instances, you will probably have accepted your invitation to speak many weeks before the actual date of the speaking engagement. But if you're like most people, you're doubtlessly going to wait until you're up against the deadline before you actually sit down and commit your planned comments to paper.

With the exception of a handful of politicians and business tycoons who have their own ghost-writers on staff, the actual writing of a talk—even for a professional writer—looms as a ghastly task. Many a speaker faces his blank sheet of paper wondering what (besides the flattery inherent in the invitation) ever induced him to accept a place on the program.

Take heart! Over the years, having experienced my own share of the syndrome known as "writer's block" and having watched many a speech-writing colleague agonize over a cold typewriter, I have developed a foolproof system for organizing my thoughts and getting them down on paper in script form. I have introduced dozens of people to my system—not only speakers, but writers of articles and books, and even high school and college students faced with term papers, book reports, and graduate theses. This system has yet to fail—provided the speaker, or writer, has anything at all to say.

For want of a better name, we'll call it the Simmons System. (For all I know, many other people may have independently come up with the same system; for it's a device born of need, perfected through usage, and heaven-made for anyone faced with an irrevocable deadline. There is no reason why The System should have evolved for me alone.)

The Simmons System is based upon a conviction that one's unconscious can be hard at work on a problem or an assignment even when one's conscious mind is not thinking about it. Take a typical situation: You agree to appear on a program some six weeks hence. You figure six weeks gives you time enough in which to write a brilliant and applause-winning talk. But you're busy. Other matters have greater priority or closer deadlines. So you procrastinate about getting started on the speech.

Actually, you may not be procrastinating at all. During the days and weeks when the project is set off on a back burner, thoughts relevant to your talk keep popping into your mind. An idea occurs to you. Sometimes it's only a phrase. Or you read something somewhere and think, "Maybe I ought to quote that." Pertinent facts come to you when you're in the shower, in a meeting, at dinner, often during a sleepless moment at night.

The basic trick, which might be called Step No. 1 of the Simmons System, is to *write down every single one of these thoughts or items* as soon as possible after they come to you. And, for reasons that will become clear later on, each should be written or typed on the same size paper or card, one item per card or sheet. I prefer to use 5" x 8" index cards because each card gives me enough room for several paragraphs of copy, should I have that much to record or to add on at another time. A cheaper but equally effective method is to tear in half a pad of 8½" x 11" paper. This provides you with a stack of sheets, each approximately 5½" x 8½" in size—very close to the size of my favorite index cards.

Now, once you get these items down in writing, some of them may not look as good, or as wise, or as well-phrased as when they were in your mind. Save them anyway. Later on, you may find these bits and pieces work well in conjunction with other thoughts you'll be jotting down. There'll be plenty of time to discard excess or inferior material when you get to writing your first draft.

Step No. 2 in the Simmons System begins when you eventually get to the point where you really have to devote some time to thinking about your talk on a conscious level. Armed with your stack of index cards, you're ready to concentrate on your topic. Perhaps the best way to start is to do some reading on the subject—articles, speeches, research, even books if you have the time— written by other people about, or close to, the subject. Hopefully, you have someone on your staff—an assistant, a researcher, a good secretary—or a smart wife or husband, who can save you many hours by going to the library for you (after thorough briefing) and finding source material for you to read or scan.

As you go through this material, you'll unquestionably find things others have said which you agree with or take exception to. Transcribe such passages onto your cards (one item only per card) making certain to jot down the source and putting quotation marks around anything you've excerpted verbatim so that you can properly credit the author, should you choose to quote him directly.

Another stimulus to your thinking will often be found in conversations with authorities on your speech subject, with smart friends whose opinions you respect, and, occasionally, with people who hold the opposing point of view to your own. As you explore your topic with such persons, you are likely to unearth new information, facts, and figures, plus thoughtful or emotional viewpoints that had not previously occurred to you. Take notes. And remember to add them to your growing file of material.

If you can't get to see and talk to all the people whose knowledge and opinions are of interest to you, write to them and request that they send you letters describing their attitudes or telling you what they know on the subject. You will be amazed at how many people reply to your inquiries with stimulating material! Bear in mind that most people like to be asked their opinions, particularly if they are to be quoted by name. One caution: if you're writing for information or an opinion, be certain to mention the deadline for receiving a usable reply.

The longer the lead time between agreeing to make

a speech and the actual date of your talk, the fatter will be your file of accumulated ideas, arguments, phrases, quotations, examples, etc. You are now approaching the moment of truth—the day when you really have to clear your desk, unclutter your mind, unencumber your date book, *and begin to write.*

This brings you to Step No. 3 in the Simmons System. Go through your stack of index cards. In the upper right-hand corner of each card write, in pencil (because it's erasable, and therefore changeable), a key word or two that tells you what the card is about. Let me give you an example.

Say you're going to give a talk on "The Pros and Cons of Legalizing Marijuana." In the corner of one card, you might want to jot down "PRO: Non-addictive." On another, "CON: Unknown Factors." Then, "CON: Prevents Problem Solving." And, "CON: Appeal to Pre-Teens". Plus, "PRO: Millions Using It". And, "PRO: Comparison with Alcohol". One card might be marked "Better Laws Needed," another, "Accommodation to Reality." Several cards might bear the corner label "Experience—Other Countries."

You might come across several cards that appear to contain good things to say right at the outset of your speech. On each of these, write "INTRO" in the upper right-hand corner. Others might seem like things that should be held until the end. On those, write the word "CONCLUSION." Several cards may contain items pertinent to very young people. Perhaps they'll get the key corner word: "YOUTH." Still others might contain quotations or opinions from the medical profession. These could be tabbed "MEDICAL OPINION." Here and there you will find a card that does not fall into any category you can designate. In the upper right-hand corner of those cards, put a question mark. (As your script starts to take shape, you'll find appropriate places where these items seem to fit.)

In Step No. 4 of the Simmons System, you're going to shuffle the cards, arranging them so that all cards with the same key word are together. Thus, all the CONS will be in one group, all the PROS in another, all the INTRO items together, etc. Clip together, or place a rubber band around each group.

Now, Step No. 5. Lay out the card groupings on a clear area of your desk or table, moving groups around until you have a subject sequence that appears sensible to you.

You have now created *a natural outline for your talk.* And it is totally unnecessary for you to "write an outline before you begin to write your speech"—which is what every textbook on writing will advise you to do. You have similar material together, thus preventing the possibility of a disjointed address where the speaker's ideas ramble all over the place, giving the impression of inadequate preparation or, worse still, of a person who has not quite thought through his subject matter.

In Step No. 6, you're going to beef up your material, flavor it, make it come alive. That's where this book comes in. Attack the first group of cards marked INTRO. Do you find in this batch anything that will provide you with your opening comment—any provocative quotation, interesting story, wisely phrased show-stopper? Do you have here anything that will make your audience want to listen? Provoke their undivided attention? Arouse their emotions? Make them laugh? Relieve the tension? If not, read through the chapter called "Openers" and see what you find that will make a suitable item with which to launch this platform appearance. If you find several possibilities, copy each one onto a separate card and add to the INTRO group. At this point you need not decide exactly which of the items you'll eventually use—you're merely considering some possibilities.

Here's how it works. Sticking with the theoretical subject of our talk, "The Pros and Cons of Legalizing Marijuana," you might copy out this item on a card: "I have considerable respect for your tolerance in inviting me to address you—and for my courage in accepting." On the same card, immediately after this excerpt, you could add a sentence of your own, such as: "For the whole subject of drugs is, today, one about which most people feel very emotional and heated."

On another card, perhaps you will copy out this story: "As I stand before you, I can't help thinking about the man who was killed in the floods in Florence, Italy just a few short years ago. He made his way to heaven and at the Pearly Gates he was asked to give his case history—to tell the story of how he died and came to heaven. This he obligingly did. St. Peter thought the story so interesting that he asked the new arrival if he would agree to give a talk to the other angels in heaven, telling them all about the flood and his demise. The newly arrived resident of heaven was very flattered, and he immediately accepted the invitation. As he flew away, a kind young angel tugged at the sleeve of his robe and said, 'Sir, I think I ought to tell you that *Noah* will be in the audience.' "

"My point is that I'm somewhat humbled at being up here and talking on the subject of *drugs*—when so many of you in the audience are experts in the field."

On still another card, you could jot down this comment, which appears in the same chapter: "I'm going to read my talk to you today, rather than deliver it off the cuff. That's because I believe it's a good idea to carefully think through my thoughts before I say something. The trouble is that it never sounds any better than if I had just blurted it out in the first place."

(Eventually, when you actually write your speech script, you might determine that you don't need all of the INTRO material you have now accumulated, and you might make the decision to discard one of these three items. Right now, however, it is better to have too much material than too little.)

In the same manner that you use this book to enliven and strengthen your group of ideas for the introductory section of your talk, Step No. 6 of the Simmons System calls for you to go through each group of cards in your collection and, wherever you feel you could use more or better material, skim the appropriate chapters in this book for additional content. *And be sure to use the Subject Index at the back of the book.* On page 406 you will find specific advice on how to make the most of this valuable tool. When you have finished with this step, you should have quite a bit more material than when you first put your file card items in sequential groups.

In Step No. 7, you're going to draw upon your opinions and convictions to supplement the considerable copy you must now have in your card file. Check each group of cards again. Under each subject category, ask yourself if you have noted every thought, every belief, every argument, every example you wish to convey to your audience. If you did Step No. 1 over a period of many weeks, and if you are talking on a subject where you have strong convictions and have jotted them down whenever they occurred to you, don't be surprised if Step No. 7 finds you with little to add. On the other hand, additional thoughts might well come to mind as you concentrate on the various subheadings that you have written on the corners of the cards.

When you have exhausted your ideas, when the core of every thought you wish to convey has been noted, you are ready to write the first draft of your script.

Getting the first draft on paper is Step No. 8. But instead of it looming as a monumental and dreadful chore, you will find to your amazement that your talk is all but written! By using the Simmons System up to this point, your speech has almost written itself.

With your cards arranged in a sequence that makes sense to you, pick and choose the best material in each group and start writing. Much of it you will be able to copy off the cards. Some of it will require amplification, cutting, or improved phraseology. Do this as you go along, adding, subtracting, rewording, inserting bridges from idea to idea.

When you have gone through all your cards—discarding those which do not seem to fit in, perhaps moving a few into other groups where they fit better, utilizing the best of your material, and working in the previously un-categorized cards (the ones with the question marks in the corner)—you will have your rough draft. And no matter how many changes you may choose to make in the last two steps, the worst is behind you. You have committed to paper all the things you want to tell your audience, and you have done it in an organized, logical sequence, adding enough material from this book to make the script come alive.

The last two steps are the easiest. And they should be the most fun, because you will be doing them in the knowledge that the basics are already down on paper—and it wasn't as tough as you thought it would be. How-ever, the last two steps, though easy, make the difference between an *ordinary* speech and a *great* one. It is this extra bit of work that separates the stars from the medioc-rities.

In Step No. 9, you're going to study your rough draft very critically and objectively, searching for weak transi-tions, dreary stretches, passages that lack forcefulness, and sections where witticisms, anecdotes or philosophical punch lines might be added. Mark each such spot in your script. Then, with each of those faulty areas in mind, riffle through those chapters in this book that are related in subject matter to the passages that need improvement. Pick out one-liners, proverbs, anecdotes, quotations—any and all material that can serve to perk up a sagging section or paragraph. If you don't find all you need in the chapters directly targeted to your subject, comb the pages of non-related chapters and select items that can be reworded or adapted to fit your needs. At this point, the Subject Index can once again be a tremendous help in suggesting new categories under which you might find appropriate material.

Let me give you some examples of how Step No. 9 works.

Staying with our theoretical talk on "Legalizing Marijuana," it would be logical for you to check out the chapter in this book on Lawyers. You might well decide to pick up and use this item: "Theodore Roosevelt once told us that it is difficult to make our material condition better by the *best* laws. 'But,' he said, 'it is easy enough to ruin it by *bad* laws.' " Whichever side of the marijuana issue you take, you could use that quotation to make a point for the right sort of laws concerning the drug under discussion. The chapter on Lawyers is, as I said, a logical place to look for suitable material for this particular speech. But there are chapters here that are *not* directly related to the speech subject, yet they contain items which, with a bit of ingenuity, can be adapted and used to improve this talk. Take the chapter on Business. One might not expect to find in it anything directly related to the "Pros and Cons of Legalizing Marijuana." Yet it contains lines that could apply to many things other than business, including the subject at hand—such as, "Perhaps our motto for too long has been, 'Don't just do something —stand there!' " This could be very serviceable to a speaker advocating that action be taken at once to change the marijuana laws.

Elsewhere in the same chapter you will find these sentences: "It's like the man who emerged from a meeting and announced, 'There is a feeling of togetherness in there. Everyone is reasonably unhappy.' " This bit would work very well towards the conclusion of the talk on marijuana, if the speech writer were to use it and add a comment such as this: "The same might be said of us. Whichever side of the drug problem we may be on, I'm sure all of us are reasonably unhappy about the current situation. Well, polarized as we may be, at least that gives us a feeling of togetherness!" Still elsewhere, in the chapter called "Advertising"—which, again, is not directly related to the marijuana speech—you will find this item: "Al Capp, the cartoonist, once said that 'the public is like a piano—you just have to know what keys to poke.' " In our theoretical speech, this line could be followed by a comment similar to this one: "However, when it comes to the drug scene, the public has been poked and pounded from all sides, with so many differing points of view that most people know not what to think. The problem is that, unlike the piano, the arguments pro and con are not always black and white."

So, you can see that improvement for your talk's weak spots might be found in almost every chapter of this book. Just keep looking. It's here, somewhere in these pages. Be sure to check out the Subject Index.

And now for Step No. 10—the final editing of your speech. After incorporating into your rough draft the new material you added in the last step, read through your talk again—*but this time, read it aloud.* Stop at awkward phrases. Edit them as you go along, until you are comfortable saying every word. If something seems unclear, clarify it. If anything seems repetitious, eliminate it. If all your sentences seem to be the same length, cut some of them and add to others. The variety in sentence length will help you avoid a monotonous delivery. If some of the words you used in writing the talk looked good on paper but sound phony or artificial when spoken, substitute synonyms. Keep in mind that your talk is meant to be *heard*, not read. It makes a difference.

When you have edited the talk for *sound*, read it aloud once more. And *time* it. If you have written a speech that takes more time to read than the time allotted to you on the program, read it once again—and this time, cut out any sentence or paragraph that does not *strengthen your thesis* or *enliven the script*. It is very important to recognize that you cannot time a talk if you read it silently. *You must read it aloud.*

While you may continue to make word changes here and there each time you rehearse your talk (even professional actors rehearse; it's suicide for an amateur to deliver a speech without plenty of rehearsal time behind him), your script is now finished—in ten simple steps, some of which took only a few minutes. And, as the material was transferred from card file to manuscript paper, the first draft all but wrote itself!

POLITICS

poking fun
at public figures
or issues

There was a time when the word "politics" referred only to the art or science of government; or, more precisely, to the art or science of winning and holding control over a government or a portion of it. Today, we also use the word "politics" to describe competition between interest groups, or individuals, desirous of obtaining power or leadership.

And so we speak of politics in business, in universities, in fraternal clubs, even in social circles. And the word "politics" always raises a red flag. For people who "play" politics outside of acceptable government campaigns are usually considered to be using less-than-acceptable tactics. Call someone a politician, and he may well challenge you to choose between swords and pistols at sunup. Cry "Politics!" when you think someone has made a statement that leaves a credibility gap, and you have accused him of having a forked tongue. There are no cool heads or calm temperaments where politics is concerned.

So, you cannot fail to arouse your audience—either to sympathetic agreement or to controlled anger—when you take issue with a political figure or his ideas. Unless, that is, you choose to approach the issues in a humorous vein. By poking fun at a political subject, you can be assured of arousing the instant interest that politics engenders while still keeping the goodwill of your audience.

Whether or not the talk you are preparing is directly concerned with politics, go through the material in this chapter and see if one or more of the items might not enliven some section of your presentation. You may even find that poking fun at *yourself* can ward off the possibility that some members of the audience will silently think you a politician. Still others may admire your frankness and grow more sympathetic to your thesis or beliefs.

¶

"The office of the Presidency," said Woodrow Wilson, "requires the constitution of an athlete, the patience of a mother, and the endurance of an early Christian."

¶

Maybe the President won't be able to cure poverty, but with taxes the way they are, and tight money, he sure is doing a good job of curing wealth.

¶

I recall something that John W. Gardner once said. Though he did not refer particularly to politicians, the application is a good fit. Mr. Gardner said that "people who break the iron frame of custom are necessarily people of ardor and aggressiveness. They are capable of pursuing their objectives with fervor and singleness of purpose. If they were not, they would not succeed. And it is sad, but true, that in shaping themselves into bludgeons with which to assault the social structure, they often develop a diamond-hard rigidity of their own."

¶

We are living in an age when astronauts walk on the moon and politicians walk on eggshells.

¶

Whenever you hear a politician scream, you know that someone has just told the truth.

¶

Calvin Coolidge once told us, "Nothing is easier than spending the public money. It does not appear to belong to anybody. The temptation is overwhelming to bestow it on somebody."

¶

Adlai Stevenson once described a political opponent as "the kind of politician who would cut down a redwood tree, then mount the stump for a speech on conservation."

¶

"Politics is the most hazardous of all professions. There is not another in which a man can hope to do so much good to his fellow creatures; neither is there any in which by a mere loss of nerve he may do such widespread harm; nor is there another in which he may so easily lose his own soul; nor is there another in which a positive and strict veracity is so difficult. But danger is the inseparable companion of honor. With all the temptations and degradations that beset it, politics is still the noblest career any man can choose."
[ANDREW OLIVER]

¶

It has been said by [the party in power] that this city has the greatest transportation system in the world. The only people who disagree with this are those who have tried to use it.

¶

Once, when Edmund Muskie was campaigning for office, he tried to explain why a small-town boy from Maine dared to take on the leadership of a country with so many big-city problems. To make his point, he told this story: There was a Texas rancher who was bragging to a Maine farmer about the size of his estate, pointing out that if he drove his car as fast as it would go from morning till night, he could just about make it from his house to the edge of his property. "Yup," said the farmer, "I know what you mean. I had a car like that myself once."

¶

Many a man goes into politics with a fine future and comes out with a terrible past.

¶

After losing his third try for the Presidency, William Jennings Bryan told this story: "I am reminded," he said, "of the drunk who, when he had been thrown down the stairs of a club for the third time, gathered himself up, and said, 'I am on to those people. They don't want me in there.'"

¶

Of course, sometimes my opponent's enemies do say the truth. Like when they tell you that he never turns away a job seeker empty-handed. They are right about that. He always gives them a letter of introduction to me.

¶

> This is a comment you might make if you
> are called upon to introduce a politician
> who is, or will be, running for office.

In fact, an introduction seemed so superfluous that I asked [name of politician] what he wanted me to say. And he replied, "Tell them that if they live in this city, they should vote Column 'A' in November."

¶

We were discussing political candidates during dinner and, with so many issues in the offing, the conversation with the man on my right and the one on my left was going so fast from soup to dessert that it was like reading *Playboy* with your wife turning the pages.

¶

One of the young men in my office said to me the other day, "You know, I have half a mind to go into politics."

"Well," I told him, "that's as good as most."

¶

The mention of politics calls to mind an argument among different professional men, each of whom claimed to be a member of the "oldest profession."

A lawyer spoke up and said, "Mine is obviously the oldest profession. It dates back to before the Garden of Eden. Surely you can recognize in the serpent the voice of an attorney."

A doctor quickly disputed him. "Before that, you remember, the Lord had to form a woman—Eve—out of Adam's rib. That surely took medical knowledge."

An engineer took up the challenge. "If you remember, before Adam and Eve, the Lord God said, 'Let there be light.' Surely that was a sign of engineering capability."

Then a politician spoke up. "I'm afraid that all of you gentlemen are not completely aware of our antecedents. The politician, I am certain, was clearly the first. You may remember the first words of the

Bible: 'In the beginning, there was chaos.' And who else but a politician could have created *that?*"

¶

As Prime Minister Macmillan once said, "I have never found from long experience in politics that criticism is ever inhibited by ignorance."

¶

I'm very much like the little old lady who was once encountered near a polling place on Election Day.

"Whom did you vote for?" asked a reporter.

"I never vote," the old lady snapped. "It only encourages 'em!"

YOUTH

bridging
the generation
gap

If you are in a different age group from your audience, or if your audience is made up of people from both the over-thirty and under-thirty segments, a witty line or an incisive story about youth—particularly concerning its relationship to older people—is a good way to bridge the generation gap and win over your audience.

Your speech need not be specifically on the subject of youth for you to employ the stories and opinions in this chapter. For example, if you are talking about the problems of business, you might want to refer to the way young people see the business world. If you are discussing politics, perhaps you will talk about the fact that eighteen-year-olds now have the vote—and this will give you opportunity for a tangential comment on the young.

You should also use the Subject Index at the back of the book to locate items about youth which appear in chapters other than this one. For example, as you glance down the Index you'll see the words "knowledge (learning)." Since knowledge and learning are often discussed in terms of the young, it would be worthwhile to check out the references suggested there. Not all of them will be applicable to youth. But you will find some references to material in "Proverbs" and "One-Liners" that could easily be applied to young people.

Or perhaps your eye will spot the word "generations." Under this listing you will be referred to items in the chapters on "Doctors," "Kennedy," and "Facts, Figures, and Research." Each of these references will provide you with an item applicable to youth and, possibly, to your speech subject.

Keep in mind that if you're talking to educators, doctors, parents, women's groups, or students, you have an audience involved with youth and quick to respond—on either side—to controversial and/or humorous remarks about young people. I'm not suggesting that you take the script of a talk on "Reversible Left-Ventricular Failure in Angina Pectoris" and try to work in a humorous story or philosophical statement about teen-agers. On the other hand, there are many talks given nowadays that suffer for lack of enlivenment halfway through. Go through this chapter. See if any of the material is particularly appealing to you. Then, with this selected material in mind, reread your talk and see if there is some place where it might be fitted in.

If you yourself are young, in either age or attitude, you will find that most of the material in this chapter can be converted so that it serves your own point of view. For example, this inscription has been found on a six thousand-year-old Egyptian tomb:

> *We live in a decadent age. Young people no longer respect their parents. They are rude and impatient. They inhabit taverns and have no self-control.*

Taking off from that tombstone inscription, you might then go on to point out how lucky today's parents are that their kids don't "inhabit taverns." Or you might make the point that things obviously haven't changed much. If young people don't respect their parents today, and didn't six thousand years ago either, the chances are reasonably good that the same thing applied to all the generations in between—in which case today's parents may be suffering from selective memory, thereby forgetting some details of their own youth.

Some of the material in this chapter can also be used in talking about boy-girl relationships, education, logic, and motherhood.

¶

An old French proverb tells us: "Ask the young. They know everything."

¶

The whole subject of youth and today's mores puts me in great conflict. I'm not sure where I stand. I feel like the man who caught his teen-age daughter coming home from a date at 3 A.M. with a Gideon Bible under her arm.

¶

There is no freedom-loving man who is not in favor of dissent. But we should keep in mind what Norman

Thomas once said: "The value of dissent and dissenters is to make us reappraise those values with supreme concern for the truth. But rebellion per se is not a virtue. If it were, we would have some heroes on very low levels."

¶

A high-school class was taken to visit an elderly painter in his studio. He had just finished a painting, and it was drying on the wall. "How long," asked one of the students, "did it take you to produce that painting?"

"Two hours to put on the paints," replied the old man, "and forty years to learn how."

¶

Youth has been very critical of the world handed to it by the previous generation. In answer to this, I would like to quote W. F. Rockwell, Jr., who wrote this in *The Forces of Change:*

"You (the young) are inheriting some 3,600,000 miles of paved roads and highways, along with all the bridges, cloverleafs and tunnels pertaining thereto. You won't have to build those. You may have to pay for them, but you won't have to build them. You are inheriting almost one-third of the world's railroad mileage and almost one-half of the world's capacity to produce electric power. You are inheriting some 2,200 colleges and universities, 7,127 hospitals, about 4,000 industrial research laboratories, 9,566 airports, 194 major art galleries and museums, 14,295 banks, 2,890 merchant ships, and 305,838 places of worship. These are part of your national inheritance. You can hand them down, with what you add yourself, to your children and grandchildren."

¶

Through the ages, men of wisdom and learning have been preoccupied with the subject of youth. In 322 B.C., Aristotle, it is said, praised the young by stating that "Youth loves honor and victory more than money." Cicero, in his day, committed himself to the belief that "The desires of youth show the future virtues of the man." Goethe made the remark that "Even if the world progresses generally, youth will always begin at the beginning." And Longfellow, in his poetry, said: "How beautiful is youth . . . with its illusions, aspirations and dreams!"

¶

Not all the motives of the young are what they may appear to be on the surface. Take the very nice little boy in his Boy Scout uniform who helped a nun across the street. He was very solicitous, guiding her carefully through traffic, and giving her a smart Boy Scout salute when they got to the other side.

"Thank you very much, young man," the nun said.

"Oh, that's all right," said the Scout. "Any friend of Batman is a friend of mine!"

¶

Wisdom can never be communicated. It has to be experienced.

¶

I have concluded that there is definitely a generation gap. We have a local high-school boy who comes over every week to mow our lawn. One day, Jim and I were sitting on the back steps, eating our lunch, when I remarked to him that I had just finished reading a quite good book about the old West and Billy the Kid. I told him that, according to this book, Billy the Kid had killed twenty-one men before he was twenty-one years of age.

"No foolin'!" said Jim, wide-eyed. "What kind of a car did he *drive*?"

¶

Most young people are also convinced of the generation gap, although a few feel they have something in common with their parents. Like the teen-age boy who told his friend, "I had a long talk with my father last night about girls. He doesn't know anything about them, either."

¶

A young person can consider himself educated, not when he receives a diploma for completing school, but when he arrives at that point in life where he stops answering questions and begins questioning the answers.

¶

The life of a young person today is tough and confusing. Most of his early years are spent listening to someone tell him to get lost. When he begins to grow up, everybody puts pressure on him to start finding himself.

¶

There is, of course, a bright side to the fact that we now have open admissions in many colleges: fewer—if any—exams, and no compulsory attendance at classes. At least when these kids get out of college, they won't have to worry about the fact that they have nothing to show for their four years but an education.

¶

Young boys and girls in school are said to know it all; and, as a parent and a person with some experience in life, I am inclined to believe that this observation is more or less true. One of the things youth does *not* know, however, is that what counts most in life is what you learn *after* you know it all.

¶

A true-life anecdote told in a speech by a business executive put very succinctly the attitude of many young people today concerning education. The man phoned home from Washington, D.C. one day and his teen-age daughter answered the phone. "Where are you?" she asked. When he told her that he had just been to a reception and met the Secretary of Health, Education and Welfare, she literally screamed across the long-distance wire, "Education! Did you punch him in the mouth?"

¶

It was Voltaire who told us that ideas are like beards. Men do not have them until they grow up.

¶

Youth may seem to be very different today, but I really don't think young people have changed very much. At least, not according to a story told by General Mark Clark about a time during World War II.

His son Bill was a cadet at West Point during those fighting years and, like most sons, he seldom wrote to his parents. As General Clark tells it: "Of course, I wanted to know what he thought about the fighting in Italy because it was tough going at times, as you know. Finally, when we captured Rome, I thought to myself, 'Certainly he'll break down and write to his old man.' And sure enough, he did. His letter read something like this:

" 'Dear Dad: It is now June in West Point.' (That was enlightening, because it was June in Italy, too.) 'I am now a first classman, anxious to get going. I am a cadet sergeant. Yesterday we beat the Navy at baseball. Last night I took a very good-looking blonde from New York to a cadet dance. I'm sorry I cannot write any more. So long. I love you.' It was signed, 'Bill.'

"But down at the bottom of the letter, there was a little postscript. It said: 'By the way, I see you're doing all right, too.'"

¶

I am often amazed by the language of today's young people. It is not so much shock at the preoccupation with four-letter words, or the frequent use of hyphenated words that begin with the endearment "Mother . . ." Listening to some of the popular rock music, I seem to miss the sound of lyric poetry. Recently, for example, I heard a recording of a song called "Winchester Cathedral" which contained this bit of deathless prose: "You didn't do nothin'. You just let her walk by!"

Perhaps the new language confuses even some of the young people themselves. I heard my co-ed daughter discussing with her girl friend their dates of the previous evening, two Ivy League undergraduates. "My date was very interesting," my daughter's friend remarked, "but I couldn't quite get used to his strange dialect." To which my daughter, a bit older and more experienced, answered: "That wasn't his dialect, silly, that was his vocabulary."

¶

One of our employees brought his little boy into the office and as the two of them walked past the office of the company president, the big man happened to come out of his lair. The father proceeded to introduce the two by saying, "Son, this man is the president." To which the youngster said, "The president of what?"

¶

Despite all we hear about open admissions to college, there are still a number of institutions of higher learning that are tough to get into. They tell the story of the Dean of one of our fine Ivy League schools, who seemed very upset one morning. When his wife asked him what the trouble was, he replied that he hadn't slept very well. "I had the most frightening nightmare last night," he said. "I dreamed that the trustees required me to pass the freshman examination for admission."

¶

Young people beginning their careers nowadays are anxious to move very fast and get in on the decision-making process early in the game. One young man went into his father's business and, maybe because he was the owner's son, he thought that he knew everything about this business. He wasn't there very long before he was telling everybody what they should do and how they should do their jobs. Finally, one of the older men who had been with the firm for a long time and held down quite a responsible position, took the young man aside and said, "Son, you will have to show more patience with us. After all, we're not young enough to know everything."

¶

Perhaps we all worry too much about our youngsters being exposed to too much sex in literature and television and movies, and so on. I am really of the belief that if a child has never before encountered a particular sex reference, then he won't understand it when he hears it; and if he has heard it before, then hearing it again won't do him any harm.

I remember a story I once heard about a little boy who was in his first year in school and was walking home at night and naturally took a short cut. On this particular route, he passed a place with a board fence and couldn't resist peeking through a hole, and he saw some people playing badminton. Oddly enough, they had no clothes on, because it was a nudist colony. The little boy told his mother about this when he got home and she merely asked him—wanting to appear interested but not overwhelmed by the story—"Were they men or women?" To which the boy, in his complete innocence, replied, "I couldn't tell. You see, none of them had any clothes on."

¶

I am reminded of the educator who was asked by an anxious mother, "When should a child's education begin?" To which the educator replied, "About two hundred years before he's born."

¶

I'm pretty far removed in age from the "now" generation. Why, I can remember when the air was clean and *sex* was dirty.

¶

Understanding the workings of the teen-age mind is not always easy.

A friend of mine who has a sixteen-year-old daughter told me this story. The girl, who had recently had a sweet sixteen party, had a date with a young man whose family had just moved into their suburban town. They were all sitting around in the living room during those awkward moments just before the youngsters took off for whatever it is that youngsters do today on dates. The girl's mother, making conversation, asked the young man where his family had lived before they moved to this town.

He said they had lived in New England. The girl's mother commented that she and her husband had lived in New England eighteen years ago, *right after they were married.* The two young people seemed to be startled by this remark, but they said nothing.

The next morning, the girl came down to breakfast and said with disgust, "Mother, you really stuck your foot in it last night. You told him that you lived in New England when you were married eighteen years ago. And I had told him I was eighteen years old. So then, of course, I had no choice; I *had* to tell him I was *illegitimate.*"

¶

You all know the saying that "old generals never die—they just fade away."

Since the growth in popularity of student strikes on campus, we have also begun to find out that old university presidents never die—they just lose their faculties.

¶

Today's youth has, perhaps, put its finger on an age-old truth: namely, that there is a difference between success and happiness. And with maturity, youth will also learn that success is getting what you want. Happiness is wanting what you get.

¶

"Youth is a circumstance you can't do anything about. The trick is to grow up without getting old. It is a spirit, and if it's there after they put you in the box, that's immortality." [FRANK LLOYD WRIGHT]

¶

Man is not born to happiness. He has to achieve it.

¶

Ofttimes, youth's hostility to its parents is ill-concealed. An old man, very ill in a hospital, told his son that he had made out his will and that all his wealth—his money, stocks, property, and so on—would be the boy's when the end came. The son grew very emotional and wept at these words. "I am so grateful to you, Dad," he said, "I hardly feel worthy enough to be your beneficiary. Tell me, is there anything I can do for you? Anything at all?"

And, very feebly, the old man answered him. "Yes, son," he said, "I'd appreciate it very much if you were to take your foot off the oxygen hose."

¶

Sometimes I think we have a tendency to put a halo around those young people who are fortunate enough to make it into some highly respected college or university.

Recently, I was visiting a friend in Cambridge, Massachusetts, home of several well-known institutions of higher learning. I accompanied my friend to the supermarket on Saturday, and while we were on line, I saw a young college student wheel a heavily laden cart up to the cash register that was clearly marked THIS LINE FOR PEOPLE WITH ONE TO SIX ITEMS ONLY.

The young girl at the cash register looked at the loaded cart, turned to the boy who was helping her bag the groceries, and said, "That guy either goes to Harvard and can't count—or to M.I.T. and can't read!"

¶

An old English proverb tells us: "Youth will be served."

There are a number of ways to use this line. If you were to give a speech about the numerous programs for youth which your community is planning, you could begin by quoting this proverb and then go on to say: "Here in our community, we agree that the needs and wants of youth deserve consideration; for, one way or another, youth will be served. Our community leaders have come up with an excellent program this year, and here are the details . . ."

Or, if you are a youthful speaker talking to faculty, parents, or politicians, you might use this line and then go on to say: "Now, in the United States, where one out of every two people is under the age of twenty-five, it becomes increasingly important to examine the ways in which youth is *asking* to be served . . ."

Or, you might think about using this item as a tag line to follow some other "youth bit" you have picked up in this chapter. Were you to use the item which says: "It was Voltaire who told us that ideas are like beards. Men do not have them until they grow up," you could follow it by saying: "Nonetheless, as an old English proverb tells us, *youth will be served.*" From there, you could continue on to the points you want to make about young people.

¶

It is important for everyone, especially for young people, to have the right aim in life. However, it is just as important to know when to pull the trigger.

¶

A concerned mother in a toy department asked the clerk, "Isn't this toy rather complicated for a small child?"

To which the sympathetic clerk replied, "It is, madam, an educational toy. It's designed to prepare your child to live in the world of today. No matter how he puts it together, it's wrong."

¶

J. B. Priestley put it all together when he said, "One of the delights known to age, and beyond the grasp of youth, is that of *Not Going.*"

¶

Sometimes, all that youth wants is to be let alone—a point well made in the old story about Alexander the Great visiting Diogenes. Standing before him, Alexander asked, "Is there anything at all I can do for you?"

"There is," said Diogenes. "Stand out of my light."

> The literal translation is, "Stand from between me and the sun," but usage has altered it to "Stand out of my light."

BUSINESS

raising your
listener's blood
pressure

Ralph Waldo Emerson, of all people, once said, "The philosopher and lover of man have much harm to say about trade. But the historian will see that trade was the principal of liberty . . . trade planted America and destroyed feudalism . . . and trade makes peace and keeps peace!"

"Trade," or business, does not exactly "make peace" nowadays. Business has become the whipping boy for consumerists and for those legislators who feel they can woo their constituents by taking up the cudgel against the "money-makers." Despite the fact that the profit motive has led to innovation, greater efficiency, and the largest Gross National Product in the world, modern business is frequently under attack, for real or imagined reasons, by ecologists, anti-materialists, scientists, entertainers, and large segments of the youth population.

Talking about business and businessmen on the platform is almost certain to provoke and stimulate your audience. If, in reviewing the rough draft of your talk, you find any opening where a comment about business seems appropriate, don't hesitate to insert one. In addition to this chapter, read the one entitled "Doctors, Lawyers, Industry Chiefs." It contains many pertinent comments and stories about the upper echelons of business.

Properly delivered, a good line, witticism, or anecdote about the business community is like administering a dose of benzedrine to your audience—whichever side they're on, it's bound to raise their blood pressure!

¶

One of our executives was showing some VIPs through the company offices, and I happened to overhear one of the visitors ask the question, "How many people work here?" To which his guide replied, "About half."

¶

What John Ruskin told us in the nineteenth century applies as much today as it did then. Said Ruskin, "It's unwise to pay too much . . . but it's worse to pay too little. When you pay too much, you lose a little money —that is all. When you pay too little, you might lose everything, because the thing you bought was incapable of doing the thing it was bought to do. The common law of business balance prohibits paying a little and getting a lot. It can't be done."

¶

Unless the cash register rings, the factory whistle can't blow. Nothing happens in our economy until something is sold.

¶

A woman on a plane found herself seated next to a priest. They went through some very rough weather and the woman, who was obviously very nervous, turned to the priest and said, "Father, isn't there anything you can do about this?" To which the priest replied, "I'm very sorry, but I'm in sales, not management."

I am in *management*, not sales. But if my telling you how to manage your company better does not affect your sales, I will be very much surprised.

¶

A free enterprise system is a system of voluntary contract. Neither fraud nor coercion is within the ethics of the market system. Indeed, there is no possibility of coercion in a free enterprise system because the competition of rivals provides alternatives to every buyer or seller.

¶

Perhaps our motto for too long has been "Don't just do something—stand there!"

¶

A corporation was about to hire a new department head, and the Board of Directors was sitting in session trying to decide what sort of man was needed for the job. The Board Chairman opened the meeting by saying, "Let's remember that we want someone who is not too conservative and not too radical. In other words, we want somebody just mediocre."

¶

How do you evaluate a business idea? I will give you my criteria. If an idea is communicated—but if that idea is not important enough, not pointed enough, not dramatic enough, if it didn't influence someone, if it was a small idea, if it didn't really make any difference to a lot of people—then it wasn't a good *enough* idea.

¶

"In the short space of twenty years, we have bred a whole generation of working Americans who take it for granted that they will never go a single year without a salary increase." [K. K. DUVALL]

¶

Because a company is rich does not necessarily mean it will succeed with every product it introduces. How many of you can remember Red Kettle Soup Mixes and Patio Diet Cola and Teel dentifrice and Hit Parade cigarettes? None of those was introduced into the marketplace by small, unknown, or inexperienced marketers. Every one of them had big financial backing. And never forget that the same company that gave you the Mustang and the Pinto also gave you the Edsel.

¶

The right kind of speech by a salesman consists in saying all that *should* be, but not all that *could* be, said.

¶

I refuse to believe that a man who is careless in small things is careful in large ones, because he has the sort of mind that doesn't waste itself on unimportant matters. On the contrary, I think that a man who cannot copy a sentence correctly is not likely to be a dependable reporter.

¶

When your boss tells you to be sure and "go through channels," what he really means is that you should leave a trail of interoffice memos.

¶

When you call someone and are told by his secretary that he's in conference, it could mean he's chatting with a guy who stuck his head in just to comment on last night's basketball score; it could mean he's gone to the gents; or it could mean that he is actually in a conference room with a group of people who, like him, prefer to substitute conversation for the dreariness of labor and the loneliness of thought.

¶

In the business world, as in the Army, when someone asks you for a clarification, what he usually gets is a background of so many details that the matter in the foreground goes underground.

¶

This is an appropriate comment for a woman speaker.

Whatever women do, they have to do twice as well as men to be thought of as half as good. Fortunately, this is not difficult.

¶

It has always been my policy in business that no fence should be taken down until I know why it was put up.

¶

Many groups—consumerists, women's liberationists, legislators—are agitating for greater protection for women in the marketplace. It is my contention that the smartest purchasing agent in America is the American housewife.

¶

Watch out for the guy who sends you a memo and asks you to "note and initial it." What he really is telling you is that he wants to spread the responsibility for the subject under discussion.

¶

"Those who attain to any excellence," said Samuel Johnson, "commonly spend life in some one single pursuit, for excellence is not often gained upon easier terms."

¶

On the subject of an achievement-oriented society, David Rockefeller once said, "The ultimate dedication to our way of life will be won, not on the basis of economic achievements alone, but on the basis of those precious yet intangible elements which enable the individual to live a fuller, wiser, more satisfying existence."

¶

Business is like sex. When it's good, it's very, very good; when it's not so good, it's still good.

¶

During the last "recession," an unemployed executive was overheard to remark that at least if you have a trade you can always tell what kind of work you're out of.

¶

And then, of course, there is the story of the fellow who shares his marketing knowledge with a bartender. This guy has just ordered a beer. When the bartender gives it to him, he says, "Say, how many kegs do you sell a week?" "Four," replies the bartender. "How would you like to make it five?" asks the customer. "I'd love it," says the bartender.

"Just fill up the damn glasses," says the patron.

¶

It is usually the case that people who worry about themselves aren't helping the business, but people who worry about the business are helping themselves.

¶

On the subject of retirement, I can promise you that you will probably keep busy if it has been your pattern in life to be a doer. A man I know retired, and when his friends asked him how come he seemed so busy, he said, "All I can tell you is that when I wake up in the morning I have absolutely nothing to do, and when I go to bed at night I have only half finished."

¶

"A 'whistle blower,' " says Ralph Nader, the consumer advocate, "is anyone in any organization who has drawn a line in his own mind where responsibility to society transcends responsibility to the organization."

¶

Many people in the work force today insist upon having what they call "security." Regarding this demand, I refer you to a remark made by that great woman, Eleanor Roosevelt. Said Mrs. Roosevelt: "No one, from the beginning of time, has ever had security. When you leave your house, you do not know what will happen on the other side of the door. Anything is possible. But we do not stay home on that account."

¶

"In order that people may be happy in their work, these three things are needed: They must be fit for it. They must not do too much of it. And they must have a sense of success in it." [JOHN RUSKIN]

¶

Innovation is not likely to come from calm and contented people or companies. It usually takes a near disaster, or a challenging and driving leader, to stimulate and inspire change.

¶

We in business are every bit as much in favor of consumerism as the consumerists are. The difference is that they want it, and we have to figure out how to pay for it.

¶

A friend of mine who recently retired from business remained active in a number of civic and social projects. One of his acquaintances had difficulty getting him on the phone. When he finally reached my friend, he said, "I thought now that you had retired from your hectic business you'd be sitting around the house all the time."

"Hell, no!" answered my energetic friend. "I may have retired from business, but I haven't retired from life!"

¶

It's like the man who emerged from a meeting and announced, "There is a feeling of togetherness in there. Everyone is reasonably unhappy."

¶

Let's not be so quick to criticize business. I really think the business community is making progress. Why, just the other day, a friend of mine dialed a phone number and got the operator. "Why did I get you?" he asked. "I am sorry, sir," she replied, "but all our recorded messages are busy!"

¶

I remember something that Franklin D. Roosevelt once said on the subject of introducing new ideas into government, and I think it applies equally to business. "New ideas," said FDR, "cannot be administered successfully by men with old ideas, for the first essential of doing a job well is the wish to see the job done at all."

¶

On the subject of businessmen who find it difficult to make decisions, I am reminded of something that John W. Gardner wrote in one of his books. "We cannot evade the necessity to make judgments," said Gardner. "I was discussing these matters with a young man recently and he said, 'I don't mind making judgments that involve myself alone, but I object to making judgments that affect other people.'

"I had to tell him," continued Gardner, "that would make it impossible for him to be a second-grade teacher, a corporation president, a husband, a politician, a parent, a traffic policeman, a chef, a doctor or a horse-race handicapper—in fact, it would force him to live a hermit's life."

¶

In the city of Baghdad lived Hakeem, the Wise One, and many people went to him for counsel, which he gave freely to all, asking nothing in return. There came to him a young man, who had spent much but received little, and he said: "Tell me, Wise One, what shall I do to get the most for that which I spend?"

Hakeem answered, "A thing that is bought or sold has no value unless it contains that which cannot be bought or sold. Look for the Priceless Ingredient."

"But what is this Priceless Ingredient?" asked the young man.

The Wise One answered him, "My son, the Priceless Ingredient of every product in the marketplace is the honor and integrity of him who makes it. Consider his name before you buy."

¶

In the days when heads rolled daily in the movie industry, they used to tell the story of the man who told his secretary: "When I get in tomorrow, remind me to find out whom I'm working for." Today, with companies merging so frequently and with the trend toward conglomerates and holding companies, we can twist that story. The man in business tells his production manager: "When we get into the meeting tomorrow, be sure to tell me what we're making."

¶

In most large corporations, one has to be something of a translator. For example, when you call someone and inquire about a matter and you're told "It's under active consideration," what that translates into is: "We're looking for it in the files."

¶

"Never make business an excuse to decline the offices of humanity."   [MARCUS AURELIUS]

¶

The last dying gasp of an organization is usually the issuance of an even larger procedural manual.

FACTS, FIGURES & RESEARCH

shoring up credibility,
or, kidding the
statisticians

If you are an absolute and recognized authority on the subject you are talking about, there is no real need to prove or substantiate any of the points you make. The mere fact of your saying it makes it so. But if you choose to make a point that your audience may not immediately believe, or if your audience is likely to include some skeptics—*or if you merely want to give emphasis to your point by dramatizing it*—there is no better way to convince than with a piece of statistical information. Actual numbers carry much more weight than generalized statements.

Let me give you an example. You might, in a talk, make a statement such as this: "Americans are really a very cultured people." Depending upon the makeup of your audience, chances are that anywhere from 5 to 99 per cent of the people listening to you might not be convinced. However, you could then go on to substantiate your point by adding comments such as these: "Seven million young Americans are studying fulltime in colleges and universities. Thirty-seven million Americans either play, or are learning to play, some musical instrument. And last year, although the sound of rock was very much in the air, twenty million *classical* records were sold in the U.S.A."

At other times, you may be using research figures in such a way that you want to admit to your listeners that even numbers sometimes leave room for doubt. In those instances, you can present your statistical data together with a comment or two, given in a half-joking manner, indicating your awareness of the fallibility of statistics and/or statisticians. Often, if you must use a large number of statistical charts and slides, you may feel the need to break the monotony by offering your listeners some pleasantry that kids even an obviously accurate set of figures.

The material in this chapter is but a scratch on the surface of the statistical bank from which you can draw information. Obviously, the readers of this book will be writing speeches on thousands of different topics, and even a giant computer would be hard pressed to print out samples for use in such a variety of scripts. What you will find here are examples to spark your imagination and to suggest ways in which a few lines of factual copy can make a point of view more believable.

Specialized books in your field will turn up more research and data than you can probably use. And a particularly good source of inspiration is your World Almanac.

¶

"Statistics," said Mark Twain, "are like ladies of the night. Once you get them down, you can do anything with them."

¶

Of course, you all know the definition of a researcher. He's a man who sends one of his kids to Sunday school and keeps the other one at home as his experiment control.

¶

Statistics are like a bikini: All they reveal is important; all they hide is essential.

¶

There are ninety-eight member countries of the United Nations who have a smaller population than the metropolitan area of New York.

¶

I can hardly believe that our country is made up of people who are ill-informed about national, local, and worldwide events. Every night, Monday through Friday, 52 weeks of the year, a total of 45 *million* people watch an average of 30 minutes of national and international news on the three major television networks—during their dinner-hour programs alone!

¶

The power of television nowadays can be gleaned from these astounding statistics: when the two presidential nominating conventions which nominated Messrs. Nixon and Humphrey to run against each other took place in Miami and Chicago, an average of 83 *million* persons viewed the proceedings over the three networks *every night* for the eight nights those conventions were in session.

¶

When President Nixon delivered his inaugural address in 1969, he spoke to some 18,000 persons seated outdoors at the Capitol Plaza. But an estimated 30 *million* persons watched him give that address on their television sets. This is not so much a tribute to President Nixon as it is a tribute to the pulling power of television.

¶

One of the aspects of television which is most striking is the fact that it caught on so fast, reached its heyday so rapidly. It took 80 years for the telephone to be installed in 34 million American homes. It took 62 years for electric wiring, 49 years for the automobile, and 47 years for the electric washing machine to arrive in that same number of homes. Television reached that saturation point in a mere 10 years.

¶

There are some researchers who take nothing for granted without proof—not even those facts which appear obvious to everyone else. I remember traveling on a train with a friend of mine who was in research. The train passed a field where a large number of sheep were grazing. "Look!" I remarked. "Those sheep have all been shorn!" To which my friend replied, "On one side, only on one side!"

¶

Of course, even figures can be misleading. We all know about the man who drowned walking across a lake with an average depth of three feet.

¶

There are approximately 300,000 babies born into the world every day—two-thirds of them into families that are poor, hungry, ignorant, or sick.

¶

The problem of overpopulation is not only one of square feet of space, but also of food production. *The New York Times*, reporting on a government study, tells us these painful facts: almost 10,000 persons die every day from malnutrition and starvation, and with food production declining and population increasing, the world will be hard put to feed itself by 1980. About 70 per cent of the children in less developed countries are undernourished or malnourished. About 50 per cent of all children up to six years old, and about 30 per cent of the age group from seven to fourteen are labeled "seriously malnourished," and it has been reported that half the children in the less developed Latin American countries never reach their sixth birthday. In much of West Africa, half die before their fifth birthday.

¶

If current trends continue, before the year 2000 there will be more than six billion Africans, Asians and Latin Americans, and they will make up 85 per cent of the world's population.

¶

Even with the birth control pill, a baby is born every twelve seconds in the United States.

¶

In a single *week*, 272 million customers pass through the checkout counters of American supermarkets. That's equal to the combined populations of Spain, Mexico, Argentina, France, West Germany, Italy, Sweden, Switzerland, and Belgium.

¶

The vegetarians in this audience will be interested in this bit of information. According to the U.S. Department of Agriculture, meat consumption in Japan, per person, is only one-tenth of meat consumption in the United States. The combined consumption of beef, veal, pork, and lamb in this country approaches two hundred pounds annually per capita, while the Japanese consume an average of only twenty pounds. However, there are some countries—notably New Zealand, Australia, and Argentina—where meat consumption is even higher than it is here.

¶

Although the United States accounts for only 9 per cent of the population of the 126 nations in the free world for which figures are available, our people enjoy as much as 45 per cent of the free world's income!

¶

The gross personal income in the U.S. is estimated to be 803 billion dollars. In 1970, the 50 U.S. companies with the largest annual sales, listed their gross revenues as 248 billion dollars. Does this mean that some 27 per cent of all gross personal income in the states finds its way into the coffers of these giant corporations? Not exactly. For the corporation income also includes sales made to the government. Nonetheless, it is obvious that a disproportionate amount of personal income does go to the "big 50."

¶

Most people consider the U.S. to be a rather wealthy nation. Yet the sum of its public and private debts amounts to a staggering two trillion dollars. This is made up of 400 billion dollars ($2,000 for every man, woman, and child) of federal debts and over 150 billion in state and local debts; the rest is privately contracted and includes mortgages, farm loans, and industrial debts.

¶

While it is true that our federal debt exceeded 400 billion dollars in 1971, you may breathe easier when you hear that deposits in this country's banks in the same year exceeded 550 billion dollars.

¶

In the U.S.A., 32 million persons own shares in American corporations. They own over 19 billion shares, worth almost three-quarters of a *trillion* dollars.

¶

When the population of the United States went past the 200 million point in 1968, that was 20 million people more than we had in this country in 1960. This meant that, in a period of eight years, we had added the equivalent of the combined populations of Alaska, Arizona, Arkansas, Colorado, Delaware, Hawaii, Idaho, Maine, Montana, Nebraska, Nevada, New Hampshire, New Mexico, North Dakota, Oregon, Rhode Island, South Dakota, Utah, Vermont, West Virginia, and Wyoming.

¶

It took the United States 350 years to get to a population of 100 million. It took us only 52 years to add another 100 million. And we will be at the 300-million mark in a mere 30 years. I do not think that the term "population explosion" is an inaccurate or alarmist phrase.

¶

Although we are only on the threshold of the space age, there are already more than three hundred man-made objects flying through space, and the oldest of these is only a few years old.

¶

Perhaps the single most striking characteristic of our times is the *speed* with which change occurs. And we have not yet reached the maximum point of acceleration. It is not unusual to read about supersonic transports traveling three times the speed of sound; of automobiles that can go 150 miles an hour; of transports that can carry 600 people and their luggage at sonic speed; or even of a rocket liner that can carry 170 passengers at 17,000 miles per hour, connecting any point on the globe with any other in a mere forty-five minutes.

¶

In the past twenty years, we have seen more technological change than in all recorded history. Tex Thornton, of Litton Industries, put together some stunning facts to prove this point. "It took 112 years," he tells us, "for photography to go from discovery to commercial product; 56 years for the telephone; 35 years for radio, 15 for radar; 12 for television; but only 6 for the atomic bomb to become an operational reality. And only 5 for transistors to find their way from the laboratory to the market." Nowadays, a product can be invented, produced, packaged, marketed and obsolesced in the course of a year.

¶

The computer has arrived just in time. The amount
of technical information available to our researchers
and scientists and social scientists doubles every ten
years. Throughout the world, about 100,000 journals
are published in more than sixty languages, and it is
expected that that number will double in fifteen years.

¶

In a single year, *The New York Times* consumes
273,000 tons of newsprint and 3,866 tons of ink. The
average Sunday edition of the *Times* contains 12 to 15
sections, between 500 and 700 pages, and weighs
between 5 and 7 pounds. Were it not for the support
of its advertisers, the Sunday edition would cost each
of us approximately $6.00 per copy, while the daily
edition would have to be priced at $1.50.

¶

Fifty per cent of the people of middle age, in the
middle class, who acquire venereal disease, do so while
traveling or at a convention.

¶

In recent years, Americans have tended to flee both the city and the country, converging on the areas surrounding the cities—suburbia. Three quarters of the nation's population now live in urban areas, but the majority of these—54 per cent—live not *within* the cities themselves, but in the nearby areas surrounding them.

¶

In at least one aspect of life, the U.S. is still far and away a leader compared to other countries. I refer to our well-known plumbing, so sorely missed by Americans who travel abroad. In the 1970 census, only 6.9 per cent of the existing year-round housing units in the country lacked basic plumbing facilities, with "basic" defined as "including a flush toilet, as well as bathtub or shower and hot piped water."

¶

On the subject of the proliferation of information, there is the story of a natural scientist in the Cayman Islands who had spent something like eighteen years studying turtles. But he simply couldn't keep up with all the new information about turtles that was being written. He would have had to subscribe to fifty different journals simply to keep up with what other people were doing in his field. Imagine, then, the amount of information pouring into the knowledge vats of the world in *our* field!

¶

Though no one questions the need for research, we often have occasion to question the researcher's interpretation of his findings. Take, for example, the case of the researcher who spent his life studying the household fly. Using the technique of the Pavlovian response, he had taught a fly to jump at the command "Jump!" Once the fly could do this unerringly, he removed one of the fly's wings and commanded him to jump—which the fly did, if a bit lopsidedly. He then removed the other wing but, according to the researcher's notes, the fly still jumped at the given command. He then removed one of the fly's legs and recorded the fact that, at the "Jump!" command, the fly did so but toppled immediately to the ground. One by one, he removed the second, third, fourth, and fifth legs. Each time, the fly responded to the cry of "Jump!" by jumping—but each time, he landed with less stability. Finally, the researcher removed the fly's last leg and ordered him to jump. The fly remained motionless. At which point the researcher wrote into his journal, "It is strange that when all six of the fly's legs are removed, the fly becomes deaf."

¶

Researchers come in many forms and varieties, and you find them in any number of fields. I remember hearing about the unemployed actor who heard there was a role open in a new play for someone to play Abraham Lincoln. He was determined to get that job, and he researched the role to the hilt. He read almost everything that had ever been written about Lincoln. Then he grew a beard and practiced in front of a mirror, moving and talking like Lincoln. He bought a stovepipe hat and a cape and a shawl, and when he left his home, all dressed up like Lincoln, you couldn't have told him from the original. He was a cinch to make it. But he didn't. He was assassinated on the way to the theater.

¶

I have burdened you with so many facts and figures in the last half hour that I hope you will bear with me while I give you just a few more, on the lighter side . . .

I want you to know it has been rumored from usually reliable sources that 196 million people in the United States will *not* be arrested this year; 89 million will not file for divorce; 49 million students will not riot or petition for anything; and 84 million women will *not* go on diets.

¶

I'm a great one for sticking to the facts. I remember hearing the story of a man who made a million dollars in oil. The story would have been correct, except that it wasn't the man, it was his brother; it wasn't oil, it was gas; it wasn't a million dollars, it was a hundred thousand; and he didn't make it, he lost it.

¶

Too many people use research the way a drunk uses a lamppost—to lean on, rather than to shed light.

ONE-LINERS

to establish you
as a sage, wit, authority,
philosopher

After you've written a rough draft of your speech, it's a good idea to read it through with this special question in mind: are there any passages where the insertion of a meaningful one-liner will help me to cinch a point, get a laugh, bridge two topics, relieve seriousness with a light touch, or re-emphasize a point without repeating it?

The right one-liners can do precisely those things for your talk—and, perhaps less frequently, these things as well: they can show that you have a philosophical bent; that you are well read and have culled important ideas from your reading; that you are familiar with the ideas of sages, poets, historians, and statesmen; that you have a broader outlook about life and the world than the limits of your speech topic might indicate.

Many of the one-liners in this chapter might also make good closing lines for a talk. If you find a line you particularly like or agree with, and if it fits in with your thesis, you might find that you can edit your last paragraph or two so that they lead into the one-liner with which you'd like to end.

In some cases, the one-liner you choose for an ending will serve you best if you use it as the next-to-the-last line. For example, in this chapter you will find the line: "There would be less sleeping pills sold if more people went to bed at night content with what they are doing to others." If you want to use that line as your concluding idea, you might then follow it with a line of your own—one that says something such as this: "Let us hope that all of us sleep well tonight." Or, perhaps, "If we follow the programs talked about at these meetings, I have a feeling that all of us will be able to sleep a little bit better."

Don't hesitate to change a word or two in any of these one-liners, if such a change will bring the statement more in line with your style. However, should you change a direct quote, don't say, "As Abraham Lincoln said . . ." Instead say, "Abraham Lincoln, if I recall correctly, said *something like this* . . ."

After each draft of your talk has been written, check it through again with an eye towards including additional one-liners. Like a bit of salt in a salad, they can heighten the flavor of otherwise unexciting, if necessary, ingredients.

¶

Sam Goldwyn once said about a chronic critic, "Don't pay any attention to him; don't even ignore him."

¶

The late Secretary of State, John Foster Dulles, was fond of saying that he was making progress if today's problems were different from yesterday's.

¶

As Mark Twain said about something or other, it's like the difference between lightning and a lightning bug.

¶

"An idealist is one who, on noticing that a rose smells better than a cabbage, concludes that it will also make better soup." [H. L. MENCKEN]

¶

"Responsibility is the price every man must pay for freedom." [EDITH HAMILTON]

¶

We all learn from the mistakes of others; after all, we haven't got the time to make them all ourselves.

¶

A diplomat has been defined as a man who makes you feel at home—even when he wishes *you were*.

¶

"The assumption that men were created equal, with an equal ability to make an effort and win an earthly reward, although denied every day by experience, is maintained every day by our folklore and our daydreams." [MARGARET MEAD]

¶

Someone has suggested that the times we live in should be marked, "Subject to change without notice."

¶

There was a time when a fool and his money were soon parted, but now it happens to everybody.

¶

Will Rogers once said, "I never met a man I didn't like,"—which is not such a singular virtue. My wife also feels that way.

¶

"We all have within us a center of stillness surrounded by silence." [DAG HAMMARSKJÖLD]

¶

There is no subject, however complex, which—if studied with patience and intelligence—will not become more complex.

¶

"We are always more anxious to be distinguished for a talent which we do not possess than to be praised for the fifteen which we do possess."   [MARK TWAIN]

¶

Prosperity is buying things we don't want with money we don't have, to impress people we don't like.

¶

"There is one thing stronger than all the armies in the world, and that is an idea whose time has come." [VICTOR HUGO]

> (Often quoted this way: "No army can withstand the strength of an idea whose time has come.")

¶

"A tradition is something you did last year and would like to do again." [RALPH TURNER]

¶

And so the time has come for us to un-quo the status.

¶

"As scarce as truth is, the supply is greater than the demand." [JOHN BILLINGS]

¶

"Minds are like parachutes . . . they only function when they are open." [THOMAS DEWAR]

¶

While the little man grabs for credit, the big man gives it away.

¶

"It is better to ask some of the questions than to know all the answers."   [JAMES THURBER]

¶

"A man is seldom better than his conversation."
[OLD GERMAN PROVERB]

¶

"Always look at those whom you are talking to, never at those you are talking of."   [C. C. COLTON]

¶

"America's best buy for a dime is a telephone call to the right man."   [EDWARD MAHER]

¶

"Show me a thoroughly satisfied man and I will show you a failure."   [THOMAS A. EDISON]

¶

A critic of our country's contemporary housing once said that the great advantage of suburban tract housing is the fact that it's junk, and we can throw it away without losing anything.

¶

"There would be less sleeping pills sold if more people went to bed at night content with what they are doing to others."   [JOHN W. GARDNER]

¶

The head of a company that I once worked for used to say, "If I should ever die . . ."

¶

Golfers lie so much about their scores that a golfer who makes a hole-in-one will often report that he made it in nothing.

¶

"Egotism is the anesthetic that dulls the pain of stupidity."   [FRANK LEAHY]

¶

Of all our human resources, the most precious is the desire to improve.

¶

To define a problem is to begin to solve it.

¶

Opportunities carry with them obligations.

¶

Though the words are sometimes angry, the blows are scarcely mortal.

¶

"Confidence contributes more than wit to conversation." [LA ROCHEFOUCAULD]

¶

An old Roman maxim tells us that "It matters not what you are thought to be, but what you are."

¶

"A great many people are perfectly willing to sit on a porcupine if you first exhibit it at the Museum of Modern Art and say that it is a chair." [RANDALL JARRELL]

¶

"It is better to have loafed and lost than never to have loafed at all." [JAMES THURBER]

¶

"A man has made at least a start on discovering the meaning of human life when he plants shade trees

under which he knows full well he will never sit."
[ELTON TRUEBLOOD]

¶

Conversation is an art in which a man has all mankind for his competitors.

¶

"You're talking through your hat and your hat is full of holes."   [THEODORE PRATT]

¶

The inequality of the world can be seen in the fact that two-thirds are starving and the other one-third are dieting.

¶

"A free society is one where it is safe to be unpopular."
  [ADLAI STEVENSON]

¶

Never forget that today's Brownie is tomorrow's cookie.

¶

"I disapprove of what you say, but I will defend to the death your right to say it." [VOLTAIRE]

¶

"I shall not seek, and I will not accept, the nomination of my party for another term as your President."
[LYNDON B. JOHNSON]

¶

Many men choose a wife in a light so dim they wouldn't have chosen a suit by it.

¶

A bird in the hand is an awful nuisance.

¶

"The reason why so few people are agreeable in conversation is that each is thinking more about what he intends to say than about what others are saying, and we never listen when we are eager to speak." [LA ROCHEFOUCAULD]

¶

"You can't fight Sidney Hall."   [LAWRENCE J. MULLER]

¶

Howard Gossage, a famous ad man, once remarked that he had waited twenty years for someone to say to him, "You have to fight fire with fire," so that he could reply: "That's funny—I always use water."

¶

If fortune has handed you a lemon, squeeze it and make lemonade.

¶

Peter De Vries once wrote that "A suburban mother's role is to deliver children: obstetrically once, and by car forever after."

¶

One of these days, a college will come up with a march protesting student ignorance.

¶

The work of the wise is to repair the work of the well-intentioned.

¶

We are now living in a world where "sell" is a four-letter word, and "profits," spelled P-R-O-F-I-T-S, are without honor.

¶

April is the month when the green returns to the lawn, the trees, and the Internal Revenue Service.

¶

As Tom Seaver told the Mets baseball team on the opening day of the 1971 Series, "There are only two places in this league: first place and no place."

¶

"We are of different opinions at different hours but we always may be said to be at heart on the side of truth." [RALPH WALDO EMERSON]

¶

There is no pleasure in having nothing to do—the fun is in having lots to do and not doing it.

¶

He who laughs last didn't get the point.

¶

"Creativity is the sudden cessation of stupidity." [EDWIN H. LAND]

¶

"Trust everybody—but cut the cards."   [FINLEY PETER DUNNE]

¶

"One of the reasons mature people stop learning is that they become less and less willing to risk failure." [JOHN W. GARDNER]

¶

"I am a great believer in luck, and I find the harder I work, the more I have of it."   [STEPHEN LEACOCK]

¶

Imagination was given a man to compensate him for what he is *not;* a sense of humor was provided to console him for what he *is.*

¶

There is nothing more disappointing than failing to accomplish a thing—unless it is to see somebody else accomplish it.

¶

"The most stubborn protector of his own vested interest is the man who has lost the capacity for self-renewal." [JOHN W. GARDNER]

¶

"Every woman should marry, and no man." [DISRAELI]

¶

Sam Goldwyn has been credited with saying, "If people don't want to see a show, nothing can stop them!"

You might use this Goldwynism as a "proverb in modern dress," or as a conclusion; or you can make it serve as a warning to manufacturers that they had best start improving their products. It can also be used with groups of parents during discussions on such things as why students drop out, or with faculty members when talking about ways in which a curriculum needs to be improved.

¶

"A free society is a critical society." [JOHN F. KENNEDY]

¶

It has been said that, with reasonable care, the human body will last a lifetime.

¶

"Truth may often be eclipsed, but never extinguished." [LIVY]

¶

There's an old Russian saying that work does not make one rich, only round-shouldered.

¶

"You have never converted a man because you have silenced him." [VISCOUNT JOHN MORLEY]

FABLES, TALES & ALLEGORIES

making your point
without sermonizing

In literature, the fable is an imaginative tale, sometimes true but mostly fictitious, which is designed to inculcate a moral lesson in pleasant garb. The moral is indispensable to the fable. In a speech, you may want to make a point —not necessarily "moralistic," but one that has some element of "preaching" or "sermonizing" to it. In order to make such a point without running the risk of offending the audience by "lecturing" them, you can use an old fable (the oldest, such as Aesop's Fables, go back as far as the fifth century B.C.) or a more modern tale that you have read, or even made up.

A good source for fables is the children's section of your local library. You'll find the oldest and best-wearing fables to be the Oriental ones; but the Greek and Latin writers were also prolific in this category, with Aesop and Phaedrus the best known in those two groups. Later on, from the fourteenth to seventeenth centuries, the Germans, French, and English all contributed heavily to the fable literature of their lands. Of course, there are also many "modern" fables in English and American literature, and quite a few translated from the Russians.

An allegory uses symbolic fictional figures to point up some generalization about human conduct. Thus the characters or words in allegorical tales signify something besides their literal meanings. You probably know that allegories are used not only in literature, but in painting and sculpture as well. To a speaker, the allegory offers a memorable way to make a point, for an interesting tale is more likely to be remembered than an injunction or a command to the listener.

It goes without saying that any tale so used in your speech should be an interesting whole in itself. There is no quicker way to lose an audience than to inject a long, rambling, and dreary story into your talk. On the other hand, a speaker can be spellbinding if he selects such stories with an eye to their applicability and to their built-in suspense qualities.

¶

There is an old story, a very durable and useful one, about the man who comes across a construction project, and he goes up to this one fellow and says, "What are you doing, pal?" And the man says, "Oh, I'm taking some mud and making some bricks."

So he goes to the second man and says, "What are you doing, friend?" He says, "Well, I'm earning a buck cutting these logs and making boards out of them."

He sees a third man with a hod on his back, loaded up with bricks, and he says, "What are you doing, friend?" The man says, "Me? I'm building a magnificent cathedral."

¶

Some Talmudic students were discussing with the professor the infinite capabilities of God. The teacher, as an example, told them about the wood cutter who, one morning, found that someone had left an infant child on his doorstep. He was penniless and distraught as to where he would find food for the child. That night he prayed to God and, in the morning, awoke to find that he had grown a breast.

When the teacher had cited the example, one of the Talmudic students raised the question as to whether it would not have been wiser for God to have provided the poor woodcutter with money so that he could have gone to the town and hired a wet nurse for the infant.

"What!" said the teacher. "God should spend money when he can make a miracle?"

¶

A wise man of ancient China was noted for his wisdom and ability to solve problems. One day, a merchant came to him seeking advice. It seems that the merchant had a problem in his accounting department.

"I have six men and six abacuses (abaci, if you are a purist), but my needs have expanded to the point where I need a twenty per cent increase in output but cannot afford the capital investment of another man and another abacus; and, even if I could, one man would not be enough, and two men would be too much."

The wise man pondered the problem for several days and finally summoned the merchant.

"The solution to your problem," he told him, "is simple. Each of your present accounting staff must grow another finger on each hand. This will increase your abacus output exactly twenty per cent and will solve your problem."

The merchant smiled: his problem was solved. He started to leave, paused a moment, and looked at the wise old man. "O, Wise One," he said, "you have truly given me the solution to my problem. But . . ." and he paused, "how do I get my people to grow extra fingers?"

The wise man puffed on his pipe. "That is a good question. But alas, I only make policy recommendations. The details of execution are up to you."

¶

There were two young men who thought they knew all the answers. They had been able to outsmart all the people in town and make a great deal of money, by fair means or foul. But there was one man, a wise old man who lived up on a hill, whom they simply could not outfox. One day, one of the men said to the other, "We're going to show that old man that he doesn't know everything, that he doesn't have all the answers. We'll go up on the hill and we'll get us a bird. We'll ask the old man what we have in our hands and the old man will answer, 'It's a bird.' Then we will say, 'If you are so wise, old man, if you know everything, tell us, is the bird alive or is it dead?' And if he answers, 'The bird is alive,' we'll crush it in our hands and kill it. And if the old man answers, 'The bird is dead,' we'll open our hands and the bird will fly away."

So the two know-it-alls went up on the hill and got a bird and knocked on the old man's door. "Tell me, old man, if you know everything," one of them said, "if you are so wise, what's this I have in my hands?" The old man said, "Why, it's a bird, my son." And the smart aleck said, "Then tell me, wise old man, is the bird alive or is it dead? The old man hesitated and then, looking deep in the young man's eyes, he replied, "Its destiny, my son, is in your hands."

¶

The truth is not always easy to come by.

To make my point, I will tell you the tale of a man who worked for a foundation and was in charge of giving away its money in the form of grants to museums and other centers of art.

Several years in a row, he had made grants to a well-known New York museum. Then, one year, their committee came to him with a request for a large sum of money which they needed in order to improve their collection of sculpture.

The foundation man asked what had happened to the charts they were to have submitted to him, showing figures on museum attendance.

One of the museum men was quite miffed at this request. "Good grief, man," he replied, "we're talking about aesthetics! Charts and figures have nothing to do with that!"

But the dispenser of foundation funds was persistent. "Last year," he went on, "you told me you needed more money because your attendance had gone up. And I gave it to you. Now I want to see the figures you promised me."

Finally, after great difficulty, he extracted the truth. The committee told him that the city had built a public lavatory three blocks away and museum attendance had *dropped* by five per cent.

¶

There is an old tale about a man celebrating his hundredth birthday who was interviewed by a newspaper reporter. "To what do you attribute your longevity?" asked the interviewer.

The birthday boy's reply came quickly, considering his age. "I never smoked," he said, "and I never drank hard liquor. I watched what I ate, and I got plenty of exercise."

The interviewer then said, "Very interesting. But I knew a man who did all those things, and he only lived to be eighty. How would you explain that?"

"Easy," said the centenarian. "He didn't keep it up long enough."

¶

I'm not going to vouch for the truth of this tale—but it makes my point, and I'll leave its verification up to others. Apparently, there was a robbery aboard the train that goes from Tel Aviv to Jerusalem. The holdup men got a thousand dollars in cash and three thousand in pledges.

¶

For those of you who are not sure that you should have come tonight, let me remind you of the old tale about the guy who suspected that his wife might not be just playing bridge on the nights that he had to work late. So one evening, when he had advised his wife that he had a business dinner and would stay in town, he came home instead.

Everything at the house was dark, and he quietly let himself in the front door and immediately smelled cigar smoke.

Upstairs, his wife—who was certainly not playing bridge—heard his key in the latch and rushed her playmate into the bathroom, where he hid in the tub behind the shower curtain. Her suspicious husband tore up the steps, dashed into the bedroom, smelled some more White Owl, and charged into the bathroom —where he flipped on the light and pulled aside the shower curtain.

Red in the face, he screamed at his rival, "What the hell are you doing here?" To which the man in the tub shrugged his shoulders, chomped on his cigar, and answered, "Why not? Everyone has to be someplace!"

¶

An American hunter was in search of big game in West Africa. He was getting close to his prey when his hard-running native guides suddenly sat down to rest. The American protested to their leader. He threatened, implored, cajoled, offered bribes—but the natives wouldn't budge.

"But why," he asked the leader, "why must they stop now?"

The leader replied, "The men say they have hurried too fast. Their bodies have run off and left their souls behind. They must wait now for their souls to catch up."

Perhaps that may be one of our problems today. Our technology may be outrunning our souls.

¶

You may remember Charles Lamb's "Dissertation on Roast Pig." The hero discovered roast pork—and how delicious it was—when his house burned down with a pig inside it.

Being shrewd, he put two and two together. Thereafter, every time he wanted roast pork he burned the house down.

It really isn't necessary to have a disaster every time you want a "good dinner"—or its equivalent.

¶

There is an old tale that dates back almost as far as Freud. It tells of a young man who came to a psychiatrist's office, and, by coincidence, the doctor had just had a cancellation and agreed to see the young man. As the young man entered he walked directly to the doctor's desk, refusing to sit down, and stood very stiffly beside the desk. He informed the doctor that he was there against his will and had only come to please his family.

The doctor asked the young man to tell him something of the reason why his family wanted him to see a psychiatrist. "Well, you see doctor," he said, "I'm dead."

The doctor had had them all, he thought, but this was a new one. "Really?" he asked. "How do you know you're dead?"

"How do you know you're alive?" shot back the young man. The psychiatrist decided this tack wouldn't get him anywhere, so he tried another. "You're intelligent looking," said the doctor; "I'm sure you'll agree that dead people don't bleed." The young man agreed as to how this was true.

The doctor reached quickly into the drawer of his desk, asked the young man to roll up his sleeve, and jabbed a small needle into the young man's arm. A spot of blood appeared, and the doctor pressed a glass slide against the blood, then held it up for the patient to see. "There!" he said triumphantly. "It's blood!"

"My God!" said the young man. "Dead people *do* bleed, don't they?"

ADVERTISING

getting the audience
where it hurts

Individuals may be indifferent to individual advertisements. A man or woman might see or hear an ad and remain unaware of it. But few thinking people today are indifferent to the *subject* of advertising, the *business* of advertising. Not only aren't they indifferent—most people are capable of becoming very heated on the subject, whether they are polarized for or against it. Those whose businesses and livelihood depend upon advertising can cite chapter and verse to prove its necessity; others, particularly those on campuses or in intellectually-oriented careers, have feelings about advertising that range from acid scorn to an almost homicidal urge to destroy the perpetrators.

Consequently, an appropriate reference to advertising in a speech can almost always be counted on to involve, or even excite, the audience. Your selection of material will depend, naturally, upon which side of the quarrel you favor. This chapter contains material to support either side of the debate.

¶

Advertising is primarily concerned with communicating ideas on a commercial basis—with a frankly commercial aim. This distinguishes it from Billy Graham's sermons, which also communicate ideas hoping to make a sale—but *not* on a commercial basis.

¶

A terrible thing happened to me once. A commercial came on, and I didn't have to go to the bathroom.

¶

I would like to explain the difference between a scientist, a philosopher, and an advertising man.

The scientist is like a man who's blindfolded and goes into an utterly black room seeking a black cat. The philosopher is like a man who's blindfolded and goes into a black room seeking a black cat that isn't there.

And the advertising man is like a blindfolded man seeking a black cat in a black room and shouting, "I've got it! I've got it!"

¶

Advertising is not a twentieth-century phenomenon. There's nothing new about it. In the early days of our country, merchants whose wagons cleared the plains ran through town shouting what there was for purchase—or put out a bulletin.

¶

A man gave a speech at a Rotary Club on the subject of advertising and advertising people. It is one of the tenets of the Rotarians that they may not use swear or cuss words. But the speaker—not being a Rotarian himself—didn't know this, and in his talk he used a cuss word he shouldn't have used in that particular hall, to that particular audience.

At the end of the meeting, a local minister in the audience approached the speaker and dressed him down for having used the language he did. The speaker apologized profusely, and the minister went on about how the Rotarians, to say nothing of the church, strongly disapproved of bad language. He then walked away.

He got about ten feet down the corridor, then turned around and approached the speaker again. "Off the record," he said, "and just between us, any time you want to call an advertising man a sonovabitch, it's O.K. with me."

¶

You might like to know the difference between sales promotion, advertising, and public relations. Well, if when a boy meets a girl he tells her how lovely she looks, how much she means to him and how much he loves her—that's sales promotion.

If, instead, he impresses on her how wonderful *he* is—that's advertising.

But if the girl agrees to go out with him because she's heard from others how great he is—that's public relations.

¶

"The truly creative man is not an outlaw but a lawmaker. Every great creative performance since the initial one has been in some measure a bringing of order out of chaos. It brings about a new relatedness, connects things that did not previously seem connected, sketches a more embracing framework, moves toward larger and more inclusive understandings." [JOHN W. GARDNER]

¶

The difference between an advertising man and a publicity man might best be explained through a sexual analogy. The man who sits at the edge of his girl friend's bed and tells her how great it was is a publicity man. The man who sits there and tells her how great it's *going* to be is in advertising.

¶

We don't argue that technology is a failure just because the production lines occasionally turn out a dud. We might blame the manufacturer—but not technology. Why do we blame all of advertising if a few practitioners turn out a poor product?

¶

Famous men thoughout history, including presidents and prime ministers, have thought highly of advertising. Here, to quote but a few, are some opinions.

CALVIN COOLIDGE: "The preeminence of America in industry, which has constantly brought about a reduction of costs, has come largely through mass production. Mass production is only possible where there is demand. Mass demand has been created only through the development of advertising."

THOMAS JEFFERSON: "I read only one newspaper, and that more for its advertisements than its news. Advertisements contain the only truths to be relied upon in a newspaper!"

WINSTON CHURCHILL: "Advertising nurses the consuming power of man. It creates wants for a better standard of living. It sets before man the goal of a better home, better clothing, better food for himself and his family. It spurs individual exertion and greater production."

FRANKLIN D. ROOSEVELT: "If I were starting my life all over again, I am inclined to think that I would go into the advertising business in preference to almost any other. This is because advertising has come to cover the whole range of human needs and also combines real imagination and a deep study of human psychology. Because it brings to the greatest number of people actual knowledge of useful things, it is an essential form of education. The general raising of the standards of modern civilization among all groups of people during the past half century would have been impossible without the spreading of the knowledge of higher standards by means of advertising."

SAMUEL JOHNSON: "Every man has the right to utter what he thinks truth, and every other man has the right to knock him down for it!"

¶

There's a new deodorant on the market called "Stereo." According to the advertising, it doesn't disguise any odor—but you can't tell where it's coming from.

¶

Al Capp, the cartoonist, once said that "the public is like a piano—you just have to know what keys to poke." Every advertising practitioner knows this to be true.

¶

A good television or radio announcer must understand that the meaning of what he says is often in the *emphasis* of words more than in the words themselves. Take the couple that had eleven children. The man explained that this was because his wife was hard of hearing. Every night when they went to bed, the husband would ask, "Do you want to go to sleep or what?" "What?" his wife answered.

¶

The man who has something unusual to offer will always play second fiddle to the man who has nothing to offer but the art of offering it.

¶

Advertising has often been criticized because it sells a benefit rather than a product. Well, I can only tell you that, in my experience, people don't want fertilizer— they want green lawns.

¶

Bertrand Russell has told us that television is chewing gum for the eyes.

¶

"Our society is not threatened by the man in the Gray Flannel Suit; it is threatened by the man with the Gray Flannel Mind." [ELLISON L. HAZARD]

¶

Britain's John Hobson defends advertising this way: "We shall be always open to criticism unless we can bring home to our critics that advertising is like the electric cables that stretch across the countryside— sometimes unsightly, always expensive to maintain, but necessary—so that someone, somewhere, can turn on the cooker whenever she wants to."

¶

What is a great advertisement? I like what Raymond Rubicam, one of the founders of the Young & Rubicam advertising agency, once said. "There are many successful ads," said Mr. Rubicam, "but few great ones.

The great ad, by virtue of the very adjective applied to it, must not be merely successful, but phenomenally so.

"Yet phenomenal results alone—whether in number of readers, or inquiries, or even sales—do not make people feel that an ad is great unless its message is made memorable by originality, wit, insight, conviction or some other notable quality of mind or spirit.

"And even those qualities do not make it great if its claims are dishonest, if it impairs the goodwill of the customers toward the advertiser, either before or after the sale, or if it impairs the goodwill of the public toward advertising."

¶

Ever since the days of *The Man in the Gray Flannel Suit*, the rumor has persisted that advertising men are heavy drinkers. The president of an advertising agency circulated this memo among his account executives: "If you people are determined to go out and drink martinis at lunch, will you please order your martinis made with gin rather than with vodka, which is odorless? When our clients see you in the afternoon, I'd much rather you gave off an odor of booze. At least then they'd know you were drunk, rather than stupid."

¶

Advertising is, of course, a form of communication. If the communication is faulty, the advertisement may amuse or entertain—but it won't sell. Let me explain what I mean by faulty communication by telling you a story about Sir Thomas Beecham.

Sir Thomas was leading the symphony orchestra in a piece that called for an offstage trumpet to sound a long call. Beecham got to the point where the trumpet was to sound—but no trumpet. He paused, then went back a few bars and had the orchestra repeat the section leading to the point where the trumpet was to be heard. Once again, no trumpet. He threw down his baton and strode into the wings to see what had happened. There was his trumpeter in a tussle with the backstage guard, who was insisting, "You can't play that darn fool trumpet in here—there's a concert going on!"

Obviously, a crucial piece of information had not been communicated to the guard.

¶

When I was a child my grandfather saw an advertisement that was selling a book called *How To Grow Tomatoes*. Grandpa sent for the book, but he found it very confusing, and, what was even worse, no tomatoes grew. I remember Grandpa complaining, "The man who wrote the ad should have writ the book."

Of course, that advertiser never intended to sell more than one book to a customer. However, the man selling repeat products will soon find that there is no better way to kill off a poor product than with a good advertisement. The ad will bring in the customers—lots of them—who will find out, after a single trial, that they don't ever again want to buy that particular product.

¶

Did you hear about the media man who got married last week and traded reach for frequency?

¶

Advertising has always been something of a cutthroat business. Two Madison Avenue advertising men were chatting over a liquid lunch. It seems that an acquaintance of theirs had just gone to the Great Big Agency in the Sky.

"Did you hear about Mark Stone?" asked one of the ad men. "He died last night."

"Good Lord," said the other, "what did he have?"

"Nothing much," replied the first ad man, "just a small toothpaste account and a local car dealer— nothing worth going after."

¶

It's a strange thing about advertising men. If you put three of them in a barrel and rolled them down a hill, one would be on top all the way.

¶

There is no denying that advertising men are often arrogant. If I were to pass one in the office corridor some morning and say "Beautiful morning!" he would probably say "Thank you!"

DOCTORS, LAWYERS, INDUSTRY CHIEFS

needling the untouchables

Our feelings about successful professionals and business people are often mixed. When we are in need of a doctor or lawyer, it's not uncommon to say "I want the *best.*" Such confidence and loyalty, while necessary and admirable, often carry with them the seeds of resentment as well. "Why does he charge so much? Doesn't he like me?" "How come he's so smart? If I had the time to study law, wouldn't I be just as smart?" "What makes him more successful than me? Did he inherit it or get some of the breaks I never had?"

Because there is often some safely concealed hostility beneath the outward show of respect for doctors, lawyers, and industry heads, just about everyone enjoys a little public needling at the expense of these three groups—especially since it's so difficult to rib them individually when you may be at their mercy! Can you imagine saying to your surgeon—just after he has informed you that he will have to operate on your gall bladder—"I hope you leave me with enough gall, Doc, to complain about your bill!" Or telling the convalescing Chairman of the Board of the company you work for, "The Board of Directors just voted to wish you a speedy recovery—by a vote of four to three!"

Obviously, anyone even marginally interested in survival is going to refrain from making such remarks on a person-to-person basis. But let a speaker say the same things from the platform, and laughter convulses the audience. After all, Doc, the speaker's only making a little joke . . . right?

Audiences which are themselves made up of doctors, lawyers, or industry bigwigs are also quick to respond to humor aimed at them as a group. While the same barb, on an individual basis, might offend many, it will usually evoke good-natured laughter when used before a group. Because, of course, it's the *other* guy the speaker's talking about, isn't it?

A good deal of the material in this chapter is interchangeable among groups. For example, you will find under *Doctors* a comment about an admirable surgeon who "never operates unless he *really* [pause] needs the money." Talking to, or about, lawyers, a speaker can easily adapt that line by referring to a lawyer "who never suggests a lawsuit unless he *really* [pause] needs the fee."

So, whether you're looking for suitable material concerning doctors, lawyers, or industry chiefs, read this entire chapter. If you don't find what you need under a specific category, chances are you'll find something referring to one of the other categories of "successfuls" that can be adapted for use in your talk.

¶

DOCTORS

A doctor had just been introduced to the audience he was to address. He was described in the introduction as being noble, kind, dedicated, painstaking, and much beloved by patients and fellow physicians alike. When he arose to speak, he leaned into the microphone and said, "However, I do not walk on water."

¶

A virus is something originated by a doctor whose wife wanted a mink coat.

¶

A man called a plumber to make a minor repair, and the plumber fixed the trouble in about five minutes. When asked his fee, the plumber said it was $25. The homeowner was aghast. "Good grief," he said, "we only pay our doctor $15 for a house call, and he usually spends fifteen or twenty minutes here."

"Yes," said the plumber, "I know. That was what I used to get when I was a doctor."

¶

An old French saying tells us that "He is a fool who makes his physician his heir."

¶

Three surgeons—an Englishman, a Frenchman, and a Russian—met at an international medical convention and were discussing who had accomplished the most during his career.

The Englishman described some delicate brain surgery he had performed, in which he had helped the patient regain his speech. He felt that he had not only saved the patient, but given him a renewed desire to live.

The Frenchman then said, "That is much to be admired. But I have performed a heart transplant and the patient—father of six children—lived for almost a year."

The Russian spoke up. "I believe I made medical history when I performed my first operation, removing a man's tonsils."

"What was so unusual about a tonsillectomy?" asked the other two medical men.

"Ah!" said the Russian, "you must understand that in Russia our people are deathly afraid to open their mouths. So I had to approach it from another angle."

¶

This story points up how times have changed.

A doctor I know told his nurse to send a blood sample out for a Wassermann test for a young girl he had just examined. "She's getting married, you know," he said to the nurse.

"Really?" she replied in surprise, "I didn't even know she was pregnant."

¶

"To lose one's health renders science null, art inglorious, strength unavailing, wealth useless, and eloquence powerless."   [HEROPHILUS]

¶

There is an old saying that tells us, "God cures and the doctor takes the fee."

¶

Doctors are notoriously impatient. A well-known surgeon, on his night off, was told by a restaurant manager that there would be a long wait for a table—to which he replied, in disgust, "No wonder no one comes here any more. The place is always too crowded!"

¶

Before he became a writer, Oliver Wendell Holmes was a practicing physician. However, it was said that some patients questioned whether he was a very serious doctor because, for a while, he had a sign posted in his office that read: "Small fevers gratefully received."

¶

"We think in youth that our bodies are identical with ourselves and have the same interests, but discover later in life that they are heartless companions who have been accidently yoked with us, and who are as likely as not, in our extreme sickness or old age, to treat us with less mercy than we would have received at the hands of the worst bandits." [REBECCA WEST]

¶

Tom Masson, a magazine editor, once said: "To feel themselves in the presence of true greatness, many men find it necessary only to be alone." There are many surgeons who would fully understand this.

¶

It is easier to like a doctor than an artist—for science reassures, while art disturbs.

¶

"A drug is a substance which, if injected into an animal, produces a paper." [OTTO LOEWI]

¶

There are some gastroenterologists who are awfully quick to suggest to their patients that they undergo a G.I. series or a Barium Enema, or both, for diagnostic purposes. In my opinion, anyone who wants to make a living folding parachutes ought to be required to jump frequently.

¶

If you asked a doctor what you should give the girl who has everything, chances are he'd say, "Penicillin."

¶

We all know that many people, when introduced to a doctor, will immediately ask: "A dentist–doctor or a doctor–doctor?" or, sometimes, "M.D. or Ph.D.?" For some degree of snobbism does exist concerning the use of the word "doctor" for other than medical men. In this regard, I will tell you a story I once heard about the famous physicist, Robert Millikan. He was passing through the foyer of his home and heard the maid answering the telephone. "Yes," she said, "this is Dr. Millikan's residence, but he's not the kind of doctor who does anybody any good."

¶

The average obstetrician is so busy that I can well
believe this story told to me by a friend who was
waiting for someone in the lobby of a hospital. Two
anxious young fathers-to-be had been pacing back and
forth in the lobby for quite a time when a
harassed-looking medico came out of the elevator. He
was still in his surgical gown, with his mask dangling
below his chin. Both young men rushed toward him.
"Take it easy, take it easy," he said to them. "You're
both fathers. One of you had a girl and one of you had
a boy. But I can't remember which was which."

¶

A man got off a train at a suburban stop and walked
over to the nearby office of the local general
practitioner, an M.D. he had never met. He told the
doctor that his wife was ill, that it was an emergency,
and that he would be grateful if the doctor could make
a house call. The doctor agreed to go, and together
they drove in the doctor's car quite a distance to the
outskirts of town. When they drove up the man's
driveway, he said to the doctor: "I know this may seem
strange to you, but could I pay you in advance?"

The doctor allowed as how it was, indeed, strange,
but said, "If you insist, my fee is $12." The man paid

the doctor and then, a bit embarrassedly, said: "I think my wife is feeling better now, Doctor; you really don't need to come in."

The doctor was amazed and asked for an explanation. "Well, doctor," the man told him, "those bastards at the taxi stand near the station wanted $15 to bring me out here, and I had heard that you were cheaper!"

¶

He's the kind of surgeon I like. He never operates unless he *really* [pause] needs the money.

¶

Dr. Hans Neumann, Director of Preventive Medicine for the city of New Haven, Connecticut, was called upon to address a youthful audience on the subject of "social diseases." The moderator introduced him in glowing terms, citing his vast experience and background but using circumspect terms like "preventive medicine" and "social diseases." After acknowledging the fine introduction, Dr. Neumann faced his audience and said: "Actually, my qualifications for speaking here today could have been given in a single sentence. I am the man responsible for all venereal disease in New Haven."

This line could be adapted by doctors in other specialties. For example, a cardiologist could say: "I'm the man responsible for all the heart attacks at Mt. Sinai hospital." Or "I'm the man responsible for all the cirrhosis of the liver in this community," etc.

¶

Most doctors know themselves to be men of science and have taught their wives to treat them as such. The wife of a doctor friend of mine went into a fabric store to buy some material for a negligée. She asked the clerk for nine yards of it.

"Madam," he said, "this is very wide material, and you appear to be no more than a size ten or twelve. I really think that two or two and a half yards would be sufficient."

"Oh, no!" said the doctor's wife. "You see, my husband is a scientist. And he'd rather look for it than find it."

LAWYERS

A lawyer has been defined as a person whose profession is to make the worse appear the better reason. And vice versa.

¶

A good lawyer makes a bad neighbor.

¶

A lawyer who was to give an after-dinner speech received a very impressive introduction. He was described in glowing terms as a man who was "one in a million," "out of the ordinary," "virtually unique in his profession," and so on. On the way home from the dinner, he remarked to his wife—who had been present—that it was surprising how few extraordinary people there were in the legal profession. "Yes," she replied, "and there is even one less than you believe."

¶

I remember that Theodore Roosevelt once told us, "It is difficult to make our material condition better by the best laws, but it is easy enough to ruin it by bad laws."

¶

The Italians have a saying that no one likes justice brought home to his own door.

¶

It is much better never to catch a rogue than to let him go again.

¶

Whenever I think of lawyers, I remember the prosecuting attorney who summed up before a jury with these words: "And those, ladies and gentlemen, are the conclusions on which I base my facts."

¶

As every good lawyer knows, it takes wit to pick a lock and steal a horse, but wisdom to let them alone.

¶

Law cannot persuade where it cannot punish.

¶

There is an old Spanish saying that tells us, "Fools and the perverse fill the lawyer's purse."

¶

Lawyers are very much like painters. They find it easy to turn white into black.

¶

It is said by the Italians that "he who buys the office of magistrate must of necessity sell justice."

¶

"The thing we call law is mainly a device for enforcing respect for custom, and the moral principles which it relies upon to give it dignity, are often very dubious and tend to change readily as the folkways change."
[H. L. MENCKEN]

¶

A lawyer and a doctor were arguing about the relative merits of their professions. "I don't say," said the doctor, "that all lawyers are thieves. But you'll have to admit that your profession does not make angels of men."

"You're right," answered the lawyer. "We leave that up to you doctors!"

¶

There are three steps in the maturation of a lawyer. He must first get on, then get honor, and then get honest.

INDUSTRY CHIEFS

A successful industry leader, asked his formula for success, commented: "Don't learn the tricks of the trade. Learn the trade."

¶

We all know that many pressured executives have low boiling points. However, in business—as in life generally—you can measure a man by the size of the things that make him angry.

¶

A man who disagreed with a Women's Lib advocate tried to sum up the role of women today by telling the Women's Libber the story of the business tycoon who said that his decision-making power extended beyond the office and into his home as well. "My wife," he said, "is permitted to carry on her illusion of importance by making the *un*important decisions. For example," continued the tycoon, "I let my wife decide such unimportant details as what community we'll live in, what schools the kids will go to, where and when we will take our vacation, and so on.

"While I," said the exec, "decide the *important* things. Like how we should disengage ourselves from Asian politics, how much money we should allocate for the exploration of outer space, whether it is better to align ourselves with China or with Russia, and so on."

¶

The trouble with the top brass in big corporations is that when men are treated as God, they begin to feel they *are* God.

¶

An executive took his secretary to a convention with him because he knew he'd have a lot of dictation and paper work. They were assigned adjoining rooms. During the night, she rang him and asked if he could come in. When he did, she asked if he would please open the window for her. He did and went sleepily back to his room. No sooner had he fallen asleep than the phone rang again, and his secretary asked if he could come in again. He did, and she said it was too cold in the room, could he please close the window? He said sure, and he did so and started to return to his room. As he got to the door, he turned to her and said, "Say, would you like to be my wife for just one night?" She beamed. "Why yes, yes indeed!" she said. "Okay," he said, "then open and close the damn window yourself."

¶

The way business is organized today is like the army, with officers of different grades and importance. Employees don't wear uniforms or have stripes and bars, so they have to find other ways in which their various positions of importance can be spotted. One way to distinguish rank is to observe what time a person gets to work. If the individual arrives around ten o'clock in the morning, then you can be sure he is an executive. If a person usually comes in around nine thirty, it would indicate that he has some authority as a manager or the head of a department. If the employee punches a clock before nine, he is a clerk or someone else with some special training. But if he shows up before eight o'clock in the morning, then he is most likely the president of the company.

¶

A good business leader should not necessarily be judged by his ability to dispense information. For today, there are many other suitable means by which this can be accomplished. Rather, the task of a leader is to fan the spark of curiosity and nurture the seeds of creativity. It is also his job to transmit the conscience of the company, to communicate the excitement inherent in the business, and to promote imaginative and courageous behavior in the individual striving for the corporate good.

¶

The trouble with getting to be high up in the business world is that your whole life revolves around protocol, alcohol, and Geritol.

¶

A banker has been defined as a man who will lend you money when you don't need it and won't lend it to you when you do.

¶

I remember reading that W. Willard Wirtz once commented, "The divine right of the successful is as false a notion as the divine right of kings." Unfortunately, too many successful men have not yet learned this fact.

¶

An industry leader, asked for his advice on how to be successful, said simply: "A winner never quits, and a quitter never wins."

¶

Criteria for judging business executives vary from company to company. I lean to the point of view expressed by Eli Ginzberg in *The Study of Human Resources*. He says: "More frequently than not, an executive who gets along easily with others, who does not fight too hard for his position, who is willing to see the point of view of the other fellow, especially if the other fellow is his superior, gains a reputation of being constructive and cooperative. And that he is.

"The question remains, however, what else is he?"

¶

One of the things a Chairman of the Board quickly learns is that the mere act of his being promoted into the Board Chairman's position has helped him to acquire a number of business associates whose principal activity is waiting for him to retire.

A Chairman of the Board was suddenly stricken with an illness that required some surgery, and, as he was wheeled from the operating room, he was handed a telegram which he managed to open and read. The wire was signed by his company's Board of Directors, and it read: "We wish you a speedy recovery—by a vote of four to three!"

¶

A corporate executive caught in the top management shuffle that followed the merging of his company with another was asked what it was like to work for a newly merged outfit. "Well," he said, "it's rather like being a mushroom. First, they keep you in the dark. Then they throw dung all over you. And then they *can* you."

¶

Because of urban problems, many businessmen have decided to move their companies to the suburbs. One

of the cities that has been hit hard in this respect is
Detroit. In fact, at a recent banquet of the Detroit
Press Club, a banner in the dining room read: "Will
the last company to leave Detroit please turn off the
lights?"

PROVERBS

letting
the sages of the ages
say it for you

The best way to describe a proverb is to say that it's a simple truth of life which can apply to many different situations, and which has been repeated so often it is accepted as truth.

For both the public speaker and the one-to-one conversationalist, the proverb is an ideal way to punch home a point or a point of view by saying, in effect, "Look, I'm not the only one who believes this; its wisdom is evidenced by the fact that sages have said it through the ages, making it an eternal truth."

It's not important for our purposes here to go into the ways that apothegms, maxims, platitudes, and metaphorical proverbs differ. (If you care, *Webster's* will help you understand the slender lines of difference.) This chapter takes a broad and practical approach to the sort of proverbial material you might be able to use in a speech or conversation.

I have not included the hundreds of commonplace proverbs we all learned as children: "A penny saved is a penny earned," "All that glitters is not gold," "Look before you leap," etc. Your library shelves are full of books containing thousands of such lines. Instead, I have selected for inclusion only proverbial material that can serve an adult speaker addressing a contemporary, thinking audience. Do not, however, expect to find here only sayings that you've never heard before. One of the characteristics of the proverb is its familiarity; in fact, the majority of proverbs are old—some very old. "There's many a slip 'twixt the cup and the lip" goes back to an old Greek myth. Twelfth-century Latin gave us "Do not throw pearls before swine." Others can be traced back to the Bible or to inscriptions on the walls of ancient temples, while still others are the "punch lines" or morals of early fables.

On the other hand, new proverbs are being created all the time. Some of them come into vogue for a period, then die out; others last, seemingly forever. Many of the longer-lasting proverbs contain some moral or ethical truth, handy to use when a speaker wants to "sermonize" but is uncomfortable about doing so. The moralistic proverb provides an excellent device for making your point while "brushing it off on someone else."

Where a proverb is characteristic of a national philosophy (i.e., typically Arabian, French, German, etc.), I have indicated its origin—as I know it. In most cases, the first use of a proverb is difficult to ascertain as it may often show up in several languages simultaneously.

Since we rarely know the name of the person who

first used a proverb, it isn't necessary to credit the line to anyone when you quote it—although you may want to state the country of origin, when known, if you think it lends some special authority to the point you're making.

As you read through the proverbs that follow, some will instantly strike you as applicable to points you want to make in your talk. In some cases, it will be necessary for you to lead into your proverb with a phrase or sentence of your own creation. For instance, let's assume you have been negotiating to attain certain objectives for a group you represent. In reporting back to your group, you have just advised them that all the objectives have not been achieved yet, and that you plan to go on arguing for them. At this point, two proverbs in the following pages might serve you well. "However," you go on to tell your group, "*when you have a stubborn mule, you need a stubborn driver. And I am just that. I will stubbornly persist in my negotiations, knowing full well—as the old saying goes—that *nothing is impossible to a willing mind.* And I am more than willing to go on trying to reach our objectives."

Or perhaps you are giving a political speech rebutting something your opponent has unjustly accused you of. You might say something such as this, utilizing two proverbs in this chapter: "I do not plan to spend all my time up here answering the charges that have been made by my opponent. But *even a lion must defend himself against flies.* I do not mind an honest debate; what I object to is the mudslinging. *If I am to be drowned, let it be in clean water.*"

Don't hesitate to dot your talk with proverbial sayings —but stop short of making them a noticeable "character-istic" of your style. Four or five proverbs in a twenty-five minute speech, for example (or a half hour's conversation) help you hammer home your points tersely, while at the same time establishing you as a wise and erudite thinker.

¶

Anyone can navigate in fine weather.

¶

The goose is only plucked feather by feather.

¶

It takes four living men to carry one dead man out of the house.

¶

Hope is a good breakfast but a bad supper.

¶

As soon as a man is born he begins to die.

¶

An old Indian proverb, often quoted by Nehru, tells us that the two greatest causes of unhappiness in man are: (one) if he doesn't get what he wants; and (two) if he *does.*

¶

He who rides on another man's shoulders sees farther than the one who carries him.

¶

When you have a stubborn mule, you need a stubborn driver.

¶

Everything must have a beginning, but not everything has an end.

¶

The one-eyed are kings in the land of the blind.

¶

The following three proverbs are variations on a theme:

If you hold hands with the frying pan, you run the risk of being burnt.

If you lie down with dogs, you get up with fleas.

He who sups with the devil needs a long spoon.

¶

No flies ever get into a closed mouth.

¶

The best peacemaker is a strong stick.

¶

There is an old Arab proverb that says: "He who tells the truth is in the majority—even though he be one."

¶

He who talks about what does not concern him will hear something displeasing.

¶

He who knows not, and knows not that he knows not,
    is a fool—shun him;

He who knows not, and knows that he knows not,
    is ignorant—teach him;

He who knows, and knows not that he knows,
    is asleep—wake him;

But he who knows, and knows that he knows,
    is a wise man—follow him.

¶

"Never measure the height of a mountain until you have reached the top. Then you will see how low it was." [DAG HAMMARSKJÖLD]

¶

Nothing is impossible to a willing mind.

¶

He cannot be a friend to anyone who is his own enemy.

¶

When a thing has been done, advice comes too late.

¶

Courtesy that is all one-sided cannot last long.

¶

It's better to light a small candle than to curse the darkness.

¶

One murder makes a villain; millions, a hero.

¶

Often, while two dogs are striving for a bone, a third runs away with it.

¶

There is a remedy for everything but death.
[FRENCH]

¶

Even a horse, though he has four feet, occasionally stumbles.   [ITALIAN]

¶

A great liar has need of a good memory.

¶

He who heeds not history is bound to repeat it.

¶

One cannot ring the bells and also walk in the procession.

¶

A door must either be open or shut.

¶

Bad news has wings.

¶

A dram of discretion is worth a pound of wisdom.

¶

It is harder work getting to hell than to heaven.

¶

A foolish consistency is the hobgoblin of little minds.

¶

He who knows nothing knows enough if he knows when to be silent.

¶

It is better to strive with a stubborn ass than to carry the wood on one's back.

¶

A thoroughly wise man knows how to play the fool on occasion.

¶

We who do not improve today are bound to grow worse tomorrow.

¶

Advice after action is like rain after harvest.

¶

You can't judge a ship from the shore.

¶

In the final analysis, the foxes all meet at the furrier's.

¶

Poverty is a sort of leprosy.

¶

He is lucky who forgets what cannot be mended.

¶

The fewer the words, the better the prayer.

¶

A crown is no cure for a headache.

¶

All are not asleep who have their eyes shut.

¶

Could everything be done twice, everything would be better.

¶

He who knows little is confident in everything.

¶

It is an equal failing to trust everybody and to trust nobody.

¶

Piety, prudence, wit, and civility are the elements of true nobility.

¶

If I am to be drowned, let it be in clean water.

¶

If you want to know what a dollar is worth, try to borrow one.

¶

Don't be sorry that the bottle is half empty. Be glad that it is half full.

¶

The man who doesn't read has no advantage over the man who doesn't know how.

¶

In the land of promise, a man may die of hunger.

¶

No one knows better where the shoe pinches than he who wears it.

¶

Don't blame the message on the messenger.

¶

Well begun is half done.

¶

Learned fools are the greatest fools.

¶

A blind man is no judge of colors.

¶

Youth lives on hope, old age on remembrance.

¶

Open eyes and a closed mouth never did anyone any harm.

¶

A father can care for ten children better than ten children can care for one father.

¶

Better a red face than a black heart.

¶

A man can usually stand his own poverty better than his neighbor's prosperity.

¶

Even a lion must defend himself against flies.

¶

Fortune gives many too much, but no one enough.

¶

Deep swimmers and high climbers seldom die in their beds.

¶

Communities begin by building their kitchen.
[FRENCH]

¶

You can't blame a man for trying to cross a fence where it's lowest.

¶

The only real equality exists in the cemetery.
[GERMAN]

¶

Profit has a pleasant odor, come whence it will.

¶

He seeks advice in vain who will not follow it.

¶

To be enduring, a peace must be endurable.

¶

Patience is the art of hoping.

¶

He is like the anchor that is always in the sea, yet
never learns to swim.

¶

He who has been first a novice and then an abbot
knows what the boys do behind the altar.

¶

If you follow the crowd, you have many companions.

¶

By asking for the impossible, we obtain the possible.

¶

He who builds on the public way must let the people
have their say.   [GERMAN]

¶

Larks do not fall ready-roasted into the mouth.

¶

He has enough to do who holds the handle of the frying pan.

¶

If a beard were all, the goat would be the winner.

¶

It is a bad well into which one must put water.

¶

Very often, rich parents make poor parents.

¶

Only a coward flees from a living enemy—or abuses a dead one.

¶

It is foolish to cast nets in a river where there are no fish.

¶

When it blows hard, the dirt is blown into high places.

¶

A man suspected is half condemned.

¶

Going on foot is pleasant enough when you have a horse to lead by the bridle.

¶

When the house is on fire, it is no time to play chess.

¶

To have lost your reputation is to be dead among the living.

¶

A danger foreseen is half avoided.

¶

Even the journey of a thousand miles must begin with one pace.   [CHINESE]

¶

If the hen did not cackle, no one would know what she had been doing.

KENNEDY, CHURCHILL, STEVENSON

quotes from three
great twentieth-century
orators

Why John F. Kennedy, Winston S. Churchill, and Adlai E. Stevenson? Selecting quotations from the speeches of these three statesmen has nothing to do with their politics.

Time was when every good speech writer considered *The Complete Works* of Shakespeare and the Bible to be his prime source books for quotable material. Certainly, the contents of both these volumes will continue to provide impressive and memorable thoughts and phrases that public speakers can successfully draw upon. But in a more contemporary vein, and in terms of passages that have been platform-tested in *speeches* rather than in other dramatic forms, there is little controversy over the fact that Kennedy, Churchill and Stevenson have provided us with some of the most eloquent *modern* rhetoric we have been privileged to hear.

235

Regardless of one's political leanings, it is difficult to deny that these men were outstanding orators and that they had what it takes to hold an audience in the palms of their hands. Yet they had little in common as far as their choice of language for the podium, or as far as their styles of delivery were concerned. But we can learn from all three, for their success as public *speakers* was not accidental. Their talks were carefully honed and highly personalized to their individual styles—even when, as in the cases of President Kennedy and Governor Stevenson, ghostwriters were employed to write the basic scripts.

There are many who would criticize President Kennedy's delivery, particularly when he was addressing a very large audience; or, as in the case of his Inaugural Address and Berlin speech, when he was outdoors and virtually had to shout his words if they were to be picked up by the microphones and transmitted to the huge crowds with any degree of forcefulness. Yet history will record a great number of memorable lines from his public addresses. The seven excerpts from his Inaugural Address which are carved on the wall at his grave site typify the talents he possessed for phrasing his thoughts succinctly and delivering them with sincerity and vitality. Those excerpts, and many others, appear in this chapter as examples of his compelling style and his fearlessness in waxing poetic when the need, and the mood, of the occasion warranted it.

But in our time, the true poet laureate of the platform was Winston Churchill. His command of language and prowess in using it surely make him a candidate for this century's greatest orator. He had a unique gift for creating a rhetoric that would not be part of the average man's verbal expression. Yet, while lifting the sights of his audience with his exquisite use of language and dramatic pile-up of word upon word, he simultaneously avoided phrases that would be difficult for the ear to grasp and comprehend. Unintimidated by the cultural level of his audience, he dared to be poetic and awed his listeners with the beauty and forcefulness of his pronouncements.

Adlai Stevenson was the intellectual's speaker. Unlike the Prime Minister, who could unite people of all classes with his speeches, Mr. Stevenson's great strength was with the highly literate. He avoided platitudes even when making campaign speeches; and, while using a commonsense approach in his speech content, he was always literate and ofttimes profound. But Stevenson was a master at using anecdotal material in his talks, and his down-to-earth stories helped bridge the gap between his own intellectualism and that of some of his audiences. He also used, to considerable advantage, his uncommon ability for seeing his own fallibility. This humility was expressed not so much in self-demeaning comments as it was in humorous stories, which made it possible for him to laugh at himself while eliciting a sympathetic response from his audience.

No matter your personal opinion of these three famous statesmen, you will find in this chapter a storehouse of speechmakers' classics: witty lines, humorous stories, and brilliantly phrased language gems, many of them adaptable to current situations.

The ways in which you can use the one-hundred-plus items in this chapter are limited only by your imagination.

If you, the speaker, have just received a very effusive introduction in which you have been credited with knowing a great deal about the subject of your scheduled talk, you might thank the person who introduced you and then say: "Of course, as John F. Kennedy once said, 'The greater our knowledge increases, the greater our ignorance unfolds.'"

Or, if you are a politician who has just been defeated in an election and are congratulating your victorious opponent, you might say: "But I am glad to have had the opportunity to run for this office. As that famous British statesman, Winston Churchill, once said: 'Politics are as exciting as war—and quite as dangerous. In war, you can only be killed once; but in politics, many times.'"

Perhaps you're the last speaker of the morning, just before the luncheon break. You might pick up a Stevenson quote in this manner: "I have talked long enough, and, as Adlai Stevenson once said, 'Man does not live by words alone, despite the fact that sometimes he has to eat them.' Right now, however, I believe our hosts have something a bit better to eat than my words."

And, of course, the items in this chapter can serve you in yet another way—as standards to which you can aspire in editing your script for quality of expression.

¶

KENNEDY

"Our goal is to influence history instead of merely observing it."

¶

"The problems of the world cannot possibly be solved by skeptics or cynics whose horizons are limited by the obvious realities. We need men who can dream of things that never were . . . and ask, 'Why not?' "

¶

"Efforts and courage are not enough without purpose and direction."

¶

"My experience in government is that when things are non-controversial, beautifully coordinated, and all the rest, it must be that there is not much going on."

¶

"We don't want to be like the leader in the French Revolution who said, 'There go my people. I must find out where they are going so I can lead them.' "

¶

"The human mind is our fundamental resource."

¶

"Today . . . every man, woman and child lives under a nuclear sword of Damocles, hanging by the slenderest of threads, capable of being cut at any moment by

accident or miscalculation, or by madness. The
weapons of war must be abolished before they abolish
us."

¶

"The greater our knowledge increases, the greater our
ignorance unfolds."

¶

"Our nation is founded on the principle that
observance of the law is the eternal safeguard of
liberty, and defiance of the law is the surest road to
tyranny."

¶

"Actions deferred are all too often opportunities
lost . . ."

¶

"Action and foresight are the only possible preludes to
freedom."

¶

"I do not want it said of our generation that T. S. Eliot wrote, 'these were decent people, their only monument the asphalt road and a thousand lost golf balls.' We can do better than that."

¶

"Unless liberty flourishes in all lands, it cannot flourish in one."

¶

"If men and women are in chains anywhere in the world, then freedom is endangered everywhere."

¶

"Prestige is not popularity. Prestige is the image which you give of a vital society which persuades other people to follow our leadership."

¶

"Artemus Ward, fifty years ago, said, 'I am not a politician, and my other habits are also good.'"

¶

"When we got into office, the thing that surprised me most was to find that things were just as bad as we'd been saying they were."

¶

At a press conference, a reporter asked President Kennedy how he felt about the fact that the Republican National Committee had adopted a resolution saying he was "pretty much a failure." The President replied, "I assume it passed unanimously."

¶

"We had an interesting convention in Los Angeles and we ended with a strong Democratic platform which we called 'The Rights of Man.' The Republican platform has also been presented. I do not know its title, but it has been referred to as 'The Power of Positive Thinking.'"

¶

"I appreciate your welcome. As the cow said to the Maine farmer, 'Thank you for a warm hand on a cold morning.'"

¶

"Those of you who regard my profession of political life with some disdain should remember that it made it possible for me to move from being an obscure lieutenant in the United States Navy to Commander-in-Chief in fourteen years, with very little technical competence."

¶

"Mr. Khrushchev himself, it is said, told the story a few years ago about the Russian who began to run through the Kremlin shouting, 'Khrushchev is a fool. Khrushchev is a fool!' He was sentenced, the Premier said, to twenty-three years in prison. 'Three for insulting the party secretary and twenty for revealing a state secret.' "

¶

"I have just received the following telegram from my generous Daddy. It says, 'Dear Jack: Don't buy a single vote more than is necessary. I'll be damned if I'm going to pay for a landslide.' "

¶

When President Kennedy was asked to comment on the press treatment of his administration, he said, "Well, I'm reading more and enjoying it less."

¶

"Let the word go forth from this time and place to friend and foe alike, that the torch has been passed to a new generation of Americans born to this century and unwilling to witness or permit the slow undoing of those human rights to which we are committed today at home and around the world."

¶

"Neither smiles nor frowns, neither good intentions nor harsh words, are a substitute for strength."

¶

"The energy, the faith, the devotion which we bring to this endeavor will light our country and all who serve it, and the glow from that fire can truly light the world."

¶

"There is always inequity in life. Some men are killed in war and some men are wounded, and some men never leave the country, and some are stationed in the Antarctic and some are stationed in San Francisco. It's very hard in military or in personal life to assure complete equality. Life is unfair."

¶

"Peace and freedom do not come cheap."

¶

"With a good conscience our only sure reward, with history the final judge of our deeds, let us go forth to lead the land we love, asking His blessing and His help, but knowing that here on earth God's work must truly be our own."

¶

"It is the task of every generation to build a road for the next generation."

¶

"And so, my fellow Americans, ask not what your country can do for you. Ask what you can do for your country. My fellow citizens of the world, ask not what America will do for you, but what together we can do for the freedom of man."

¶

"Let both sides explore what problems unite us instead of belaboring those problems which divide us."

¶

"The farmer is the only man in our economy who buys everything he buys at retail, sells everything he sells at wholesale, and pays the freight both ways."

¶

"In the long history of the world only a few generations have been granted the role of defending freedom in its hour of maximum danger. I do not shrink from this responsibility. I welcome it."

¶

"Now the trumpet summons us again, not as a call to bear arms, though arms we need; not as a call to battle, though embattled we are; but as a call to bear the burden of a long twilight struggle, a struggle against the common enemies of man—tyranny, poverty, disease, and war itself."

¶

"On the Presidential coat of arms, the American eagle holds in his right talon the olive branch, while in his left is a bundle of arrows. We intend to give equal attention to both."

¶

President Kennedy and Premier Khrushchev were discussing the nuclear test ban. President Kennedy made a point by using a Chinese proverb, which states that "The journey of a thousand miles begins with one step." "You seem to know the Chinese," replied Khrushchev. To which President Kennedy replied, "We may both get to know them better."

¶

"Children are the world's most valuable resource and its best hope for the future."

¶

"If we cannot end now our differences, at least we can help make the world safe for diversity. For in the final analysis, our most basic common link is that we all inherit this planet. We all breathe the same air. We all cherish our children's future. And we are all mortal."

¶

"Let every nation know, whether it wishes us well or ill, that we shall pay any price, bear any burden, meet any hardship, support any friend, oppose any foe to assure the survival and the success of liberty."

¶

"We hold the view that the people come first, not the government."

¶

Officiating at a ceremony where he was to pull a switch that would activate generators located more than a hundred miles away, President Kennedy commented: "I never know when I press these whether I am going to blow up Massachusetts or start the project."

¶

"No government is better than the men who compose it."

¶

"We believe that our society is the best, but that does not mean that it automatically survives."

¶

"Change is the law of life. And those who look only to the past are certain to miss the future."

¶

"Things do not happen. They are made to happen."

¶

"I am concerned with what is on the other side of the moon, but I am also concerned with the condition of life of the man or woman on the other side of the street."

¶

"A man may die, nations may rise and fall, but an idea lives on. Ideas have endurance without death."

CHURCHILL

"I always avoid prophesying beforehand, because it is much better policy to prophesy after the event has already taken place."

¶

"Civilization will not last, freedom will not survive, peace will not be kept, unless a very large majority of mankind unite together to defend them and show themselves possessed of a constabulary power before which barbaric and atavistic forces will stand in awe."

¶

After the battle of Dunkirk, in addressing the House of
Commons, Mr. Churchill said: "We shall go on to the
end . . . we shall fight on the seas and oceans, we shall
fight with growing confidence and growing strength in
the air. We shall defend our island, whatever the cost
may be. We shall fight on the beaches, we shall fight
on the landing-grounds, we shall fight in the fields and
in the streets, we shall fight in the hills. We shall never
surrender . . ."

¶

"Everyone has his day and some days last longer than
others."

¶

"Can peace, good will and confidence be built upon
submission to wrongdoing backed by force? One may
put this question in the largest form. Has any benefit
or progress ever been achieved by the human race by
submission to organized and calculated violence? As we
look back over the long story of the nations, we must
see that, on the contrary, their glory has been founded
upon the spirit of resistance to tyranny and injustice,
especially when these evils seemed to be backed by
heavier force."

¶

Churchill referred to the British victory at Dunkirk as "A miracle of deliverance, achieved by valor, by perseverance, by perfect discipline, by faultless service, by resource, by skill, by unconquerable fidelity . . ."

¶

"I am always ready to learn, although I do not always like being taught."

¶

"Why is it that from so many lands men look towards us today? It is certainly not because we have gained advantages in a race of armaments, or have scored a point by some deeply planned diplomatic intrigue, or because we exhibit the blatancy and terrorism of ruthless power. It is because we stand on the side of the general need."

¶

"Any clever person can make plans for winning a war if he has no responsibility for carrying them out."

¶

"Death and sorrow will be the companions of our journey; hardship our garment; constancy and valor our only shield. We must be united, we must be undaunted, we must be inflexible. Our qualities and deeds must burn and glow through the gloom of Europe until they become the veritable beacon of its salvation."

¶

"A fanatic is one who can't change his mind and won't change the subject."

¶

"There are two supreme obligations which rest upon a government. They are of equal importance. One is to strive to prevent war, and the other is to be ready if war should come."

¶

"Hate is a bad guide."

¶

In commenting on dictators, Winston S. Churchill had
this to say: "They are afraid of words and thoughts:
words spoken abroad, thoughts stirring at home . . .
terrify them. A little mouse of thought appears in the
room, and even the mightiest potentates are thrown
into panic. They make frantic efforts to bar out
thoughts and words; they are afraid of the workings of
the human mind. Cannons, aeroplanes, they can
manufacture in large quantities; but how are they to
quell the natural promptings of human nature, which
after all these centuries of trial and progress has
inherited a whole armory of potent and indestructible
knowledge?"

¶

"Politics are as exciting as war—and quite as
dangerous. In war, you can only be killed once but in
politics, many times."

¶

"I am certainly not one of those who need to be
prodded. In fact, if anything, I am a prod."

¶

In commenting upon the horror that English-speaking people have for the one-man power of dictatorships, Winston Churchill said: "They are quite ready to follow a leader for a time, as long as he is serviceable to them; but the idea of handing themselves over, lock, stock and barrel, body and soul, to one man, and worshiping him as if he were an idol—that has always been odious to the whole theme and nature of our civilization."

¶

"I have always earned my living by the pen and by my tongue."

¶

Mr. Churchill defined democracy as "The occasional necessity of deferring to the opinions of others."

¶

"The day will come when the joybells will ring again throughout Europe, and when victorious nations, masters not only of their foes but of themselves, will plan and build in justice, in tradition, and in freedom a house of many mansions where there will be room for all."

¶

"I have derived continued benefit from criticism at all periods of my life, and I do not remember any time when I was ever short of it."

¶

"I have nothing to offer but blood, toil, tears, and sweat."

¶

Winston Churchill was modest on the subject of the important role he played in inspiring his nation during the second World War. "It was the nation and the race dwelling around the globe," he said, "that had the lion's heart. I had the luck to be called upon to give the roar. I also hope I sometimes suggested to the lion the right place to use his claws."

¶

"I have always urged fighting wars and other contentions with might and main till overwhelming victory, and then offering the hand of friendship to the vanquished."

¶

"If the British Empire is fated to pass from life into history, we must hope it will not be by the slow processes of dispersion and decay, but in some supreme exertion for freedom, for right and for truth."

¶

"Come then: let us to the task, to the battle, to the toil —each to our part, each to our station. Fill the armies, rule the air, pour out the munitions, strangle the U-boats, sweep the mines, plow the land, build the ships, guard the streets, succor the wounded, uplift the downcast, and honor the brave. Let us go forward together. . . . There is not a week, nor a day, nor an hour to lose."

¶

"I am ready to meet my Maker. Whether my Maker is prepared for the great ordeal of meeting me is another matter."

STEVENSON

"We must be on our guard against the danger . . . of confusing pronouncements with reality and proclamations with policy. For these are the ingredients of extremist opinion."

¶

"Progress is what happens when impossibility yields to necessity."

¶

In replying to a criticism that he used wit which was too "highbrow" in his speeches, Stevenson said: "If it is a crime to trust the people's common sense and native intelligence, I gladly plead guilty. I've just been trying to give the customers the right change. That seems to be novel and effete."

¶

Adlai Stevenson once suggested a proposal be made to the Republican Party. "If they will stop telling lies about the Democrats," he said, "I will stop telling the truth about them."

¶

"If we have the courage and the fortitude to walk through the valley of the shadow boldly and mercifully and justly, we shall yet emerge in the blazing dawn of a glorious new day."

¶

In making reference to the fact that he sometimes did not know when to stop talking and that he sometimes talked interminably, Stevenson said: "I am a little like the girl in school who was asked to spell 'banana,' and she said, 'I can spell banana, but I never know when to stop.'"

¶

"They say I am a captive of the city bosses, then of the CIO, and then of the Dixiecrats, and then of Wall

Street, and then of an organization called ADA. Next week, I'll probably read in the papers that I am the captive of a girl named Ada. I have not met her yet, I had no idea I was so popular, and I hope I can bear this multiple courtship and captivity with becoming modesty."

¶

Adlai Stevenson, deeply grieved by the death of his good friend Eleanor Roosevelt, said this: "Yesterday I said I had lost more than a friend; I had lost an inspiration. She would rather light candles than curse the darkness, and her glow has warmed the world."

¶

When President Kennedy appointed to office several men from Adlai Stevenson's Chicago law firm, Mr. Stevenson remarked: "I regret that I have but one law firm to give to my country."

¶

"We are trying to construct a civilized world for . . . man. . . . This aim may appear one of high generality. But so are such phrases as the 'defense of national interest' . . . or 'the white man's burden,' or any of the

other catch phrases with which men have gone out
with good conscience to plunder and maim their
neighbors."

¶

In conversing with a friend who had just been
appointed to a new post, Adlai Stevenson was heard to
have said: "Congratulations on your election as
president. I know from hearsay how satisfying that
can be."

¶

"Those who benefit by the vested privileges or
injustices of an existing order always resent and resist
change."

¶

". . . I've decided that I could have no better epitaph
than 'the man who put "candid" in candidate.' "

¶

On accepting the Presidential nomination of the
Democratic Party in 1952, Governor Stevenson said:

"When the tumult and the shouting die, when the bands are gone and the lights are dimmed, there is the stark responsibility in an hour of history haunted with those gaunt, grim specters of strife, dissension, and ruthless, inscrutable, and hostile power abroad."

¶

"I am not sure what it means when one says he is a conservative in fiscal affairs and a liberal in human affairs. I assume what it means is that you will strongly recommend the building of a great many schools to accommodate the needs of our children, but not provide the money."

¶

"Man does not live by words alone, despite the fact that sometimes he has to eat them."

¶

After his defeat in the 1952 presidential campaign, Adlai Stevenson commented in an address to a group of reporters: "I have great faith in the people. As to their wisdom, well, Coca-Cola still outsells champagne."

¶

In his eulogy for Eleanor Roosevelt, Mr. Stevenson described her as ". . . a woman who spoke for the good toward which man aspires, in a world which has seen too much of the evil of which man is capable."

¶

During the Cuban missile crisis in 1962, the Russians argued that the threat to peace had been caused, not by the Soviet Union in secretly installing weapons in Cuba, but by the United States. To which Mr. Stevenson replied, "This is the first time that I have ever heard it said that the crime is not the burglary, but the discovery of the burglar."

¶

"I believe with all my heart that those who would beguile the voters by lies or half-truths, or corrupt them by fear and falsehood, are committing spiritual treason against our institutions. They are doing the work of our enemies."

¶

"A funny thing happened to me on the way to the White House . . ."

¶

"I pray that the imagination we unlock for defense and arms and outer space may be unlocked as well for grace and beauty in our daily lives. As an economy, we need it. As a society, we shall perish without it."

¶

Adlai Stevenson was once late in arriving at an affair where he was scheduled to give a talk. It seems that he had been held up by a military parade. He explained this to his audience and then went on to remark: "Military heroes are always getting in my way."

¶

". . . we Americans do not fear the winds of change and the winds of freedom which are blowing across so much of the world. To us they make a wonderful sound; and as the seeds they carry take root and grow, we will feel that America's great purpose in this world is being fulfilled."

¶

"That which unites us as American citizens is far greater than that which divides us as political parties."

¶

"We travel together, passengers on a little spaceship, dependent on its vulnerable supplies of air and soil . . . preserved from annihilation only by the care, the work, and I will say the love, we give our fragile craft."

¶

"Every man has a right to be heard. But no man has the right to strangle democracy with a single set of vocal cords."

¶

"I utterly reject the argument that we ought to grant all men their rights just because if we do not, we shall give Soviet Russia a propaganda weapon. This concept is itself tainted with Communist wiliness. It insultingly infers that were it not for the Communists, we would not do what is right. The answer to this argument is that we must do what is right for right's sake alone."

¶

"The sound of tireless voices is the price we pay for the right to hear the music of our own opinions."

¶

"It is only by intense thought, by great effort, by burning idealism and unlimited sacrifice that freedom has prevailed. And the efforts which were first necessary to create it are fully as necessary to sustain it in our own day."

¶

"Freedom and security are indivisible and . . . any society which chooses one, loses both."

¶

"My opponents say that America cannot afford to be strong. I say that America cannot afford to be weak."

¶

"This confusion over who is doing what to whom makes me think of the schoolboy who came home with his face damaged and his clothes torn, and when his mother asked him how the fight had started, he said: 'It started when the other guy hit me back.'"

¶

"No nation, however powerful, can subdue all the tides of history to its will."

¶

"I say to you that the anatomy of patriotism is complex. But surely intolerance and public irresponsibility cannot be cloaked in the shining armor of rectitude and of righteousness. Nor can the denial of the right to hold ideas that are different—the freedom of man to think as he pleases. To strike freedom of the mind with the fist of patriotism is an old and ugly subtlety."

¶

After losing to Eisenhower in 1952, Adlai Stevenson remarked: "I felt like a little boy who had stubbed his toe in the dark. He was too old to cry, but it hurt too much to laugh."

¶

"My predicament reminds me of the little boy in the radio contest. He was asked to tell, in twenty-five words or less, why he liked this particular program. After considerable effort at finding the most impressive argument he could muster, the boy uttered this testimonial: 'I like the Jack Smith Show because as soon as it's over the Lone Ranger comes on.' "

¶

"Let us proclaim our faith in the future of man. Of good heart and good cheer, faithful to ourselves and our traditions, we can lift the cause of freedom, the cause of free men, so high no power on earth can tear it down."

¶

"Our prayer is that men everywhere will learn, finally, to live as brothers, to respect each other's differences, to heal each other's wounds, to promote each other's progress, and to benefit from each other's knowledge."

¶

"No one can be certain about the meaning of peace. But we all can be certain about the meaning of war."

WISDOM
OF THE EAST

from India and China,
101 worldly comments
on life

In their centuries-long quest for the meaning of life, Indian and Chinese writers, philosophers, seers, poets, teachers and astrologers have made bounteous contributions to the world in the form of pithy expressions which are as relevant and sagacious today as they were hundreds and even thousands of years ago. This rich treasury of wisdom offers you, in your role of public speaker, an opportunity to present to your audience philosophical and worldly points of view, phrased in succinct and readily understandable language.

The Western world's growing interest in Indian gurus and Chinese philosophers has gained momentum in recent years and audiences grow uncommonly attentive when a speaker supports or summarizes his beliefs with quotations drawn from the wisdom of the East. This chapter contains material as old as Confucius and as contemporary as Mao Tse-tung, but its beauty lies in the fact that even a fourth-century saying: "The tail of China is large and will not be wagged" might have been uttered yesterday; and a thousand-year-old toast: "May you live in interesting times!" will prove as serviceable at your next cocktail party as when it was first used.

The pragmatic philosophies of India and China both concentrate on day-to-day, worldly wisdom, suggesting interpretations of life and telling us how best to live it. In the case of India, Western attitudes toward her contributions to world civilization have not always been generous. Yet, in addition to the philosophy of Buddhism with its emphasis on self-examination and inquiry, we owe to India, particularly to the creative Hindu mind, a great deal of imaginative literature including the origins of animal fables as we know them and many of our own popular childhood fairy tales. From both Hinduism and Buddhism come the philosophy of non-violence and the rejection of materialism.

Many of the sayings given here are characterized by Hindu morality and mirror the ethos and folklore of the people. While this Indian wisdom, passed down both through the literature and from father to son, searches for a way of life that will provide peace of mind, the Chinese philosophies, particularly those stemming from Confucianism, concentrate on human values and human relationships. Through the centuries, most of the philosophy —non-mystical, enduring, humanistic—has been inseparable from matters of personal conduct.

The Chinese do not strive for originality, but, rather, seek eternal truths which are reflected in the philosophical attitudes of the people and in their adherence to older and more traditional ways of looking at things. Of course, we must expect that some of this will change with the new order, even though the indications are that much of the ancient Chinese philosophy is still being quoted today.

You need not be giving a speech about the East to use the material in this chapter. No matter what the subject of your planned talk, read these 101 comments. One or more of them may well serve to summarize or urge upon listeners a point of view you wish to convey, and permit you to do it in a style which is erudite, concise, and of contemporary interest. Since some of the comments that follow have the flavor of proverbs, you will find it helpful if you re-read the section which opens the chapter on Proverbs.

There is no need to justify to the audience your use of Eastern logic, particularly nowadays. People associate "wise sayings" with the Chinese and also, if to a lesser degree, with the teachings of the Indian guru or pundit. However, should time permit, and should you feel that you want to relieve a serious moment with a light touch, there is a delightful story with which you can follow up your use of any of the material in this chapter and, in so doing, explain why you have looked to the East to make your point.

If you have used a Chinese quotation you might lead into the story this way: "Whatever opinion you may have of the People's Republic, I'm sure you'll agree that Chinese knowledge and wisdom are admirable. Which puts me in mind of a story I heard just the other day . . ."

If you have used an Indian selection from this chap-

ter you might bridge to your story in a manner such as this: "When one thinks about some of the wisdom we have garnered from the Hindus, it's easy to understand why so many great men—including Goethe and Schopenhauer—found inspiration in Indian philosophies. Sometimes, I think, we have a tendency to forget how much knowledge came to the Western world from the East. Which reminds me of a story I heard the other day about *China*—another Eastern country where wisdom is much admired . . ."

And then you can tell this story: A man in Connecticut wanted to go to the People's Republic of China. He went to the East Norwalk railroad station and asked the clerk for a ticket to Peking. "We wouldn't have a Peking ticket here," the clerk told him. "We're just a small commuter station. Why don't you try the station at South Norwalk, which is much larger?" So the man went to South Norwalk and asked the clerk for a ticket to Peking. "Peking?" repeated the clerk, "Let me see if we go there." He checked his schedules. "Nope," he said, "we go to Greenwich and Stamford but not to Peking." Then, scratching his head, he said, "You might be able to get it at Grand Central Station in New York City. That's the biggest railroad center in the East."

So the man went to Grand Central Station, and he waited a long time in line, and when he got to the window he asked the man for a ticket to Peking. "Forget it!" said the clerk. "We don't get any of the good trains out of here. They get 'em all out of Penn Station, on the other side of the city. Maybe you should try there."

So the man went to Penn Station and when he asked for a ticket to Peking the clerk said, "We don't have it and

I can assure you that you won't get it anywhere around here. The only place you're going to get a railroad ticket to Peking is in Moscow." So the man flew to Moscow and went to the railroad and asked for a ticket to Peking and he got it. Off to the People's Republic of China he went, and he spent a couple of weeks sight-seeing and doing some business and when he was ready to go home he went to the railroad station in Peking and asked the clerk for a ticket to Norwalk, Connecticut. "Yes indeed," said the Chinese ticket clerk. "*East* Norwalk or *South* Norwalk?"

And now, to add a philosophical flavor to your speech, here are a hundred and one bits of wisdom from the East . . .

¶

FROM INDIA

Sarcasam is the last weapon of the defeated wit.

¶

Learn to be careful of what you say. That which goes out of your mouth goes into someone's ear.

¶

It is possible to buy brains and muscle. But you cannot buy loyalty, which can only be earned.

¶

Life is not a continuum of pleasant, elective choices,
but of inevitable problems that call for strength,
determination and hard work.

¶

When a man says he would like to do good for
humanity, ask him how well he gets on with his family.

¶

The reason more progress is not made in the
improvement of the human race is that the improvers
do not all begin with themselves.

¶

A word to the wise is sufficient, but a word to the
foolish is often one too many.

¶

Though a gem be cast into the dirt, its purity cannot
be sullied; though a good man lives in a vile place, his
heart cannot be depraved.

¶

In lighting a candle, we seek light to illuminate a dark chamber. In reading a book, we seek for reason to enlighten the heart.

¶

When a man obtains a large sum without having earned it, if it does not make him very happy, it will certainly make him very miserable.

¶

Truth crushed to earth will rise again, but it takes its time in doing so and error gets in a great deal of mischief meanwhile. Thus, all good people should labor to keep truth on its feet.

¶

Kindness is never wasted. If it has no effect on the recipient, at least it benefits the bestower.

¶

Though your fields yield many bushels of corn, you can eat but a pint a day; though your house be ever so large, you can sleep on but eight feet at night.

¶

If you long for wealth and position, ask whether you are willing to work yourself to death for it.

¶

Virtue beautifies.

¶

Given three men with equal skill, he who plays for the sake of the game will play well. He who stakes his daughter, will be nervous. And he who plays for gold, will lose his wits.

¶

Should you find that your well-meant counsels are not heeded, depart quietly.

¶

The great man usually stands apart from the crowd. But part of his greatness is that he takes no credit for his exceptionality.

¶

Perfect trust requires no pledges.

¶

The masses value money; honest men, fame; virtuous men, resolution; and sages, the soul.

¶

Too many men seek ways to spend their leisure when they have not yet learned to adapt themselves to the natural conditions of their existence.

¶

If a man dies for charity and duty to his neighbor, the world calls him noble. If he dies for gain, the world calls him lowly. The dying is the same; it is up to you to choose your path to it.

¶

Only from subjective knowledge is it possible to proceed to objective knowledge.

¶

Speech is not mere breath. It is supposed to have meaning. Take away that and you cannot distinguish it from the chirping of birds.

¶

You don't ask a blind man's opinion of a picture, nor do you invite a deaf man to a concert. But blindness and deafness are not only physical. There is a blindness and deafness of the mind as well. You should not, therefore, ask those afflicted with such infirmities to discuss philosophies with you.

¶

As a man in a dream can form a thousand sorts of shapes, so by contemplation is the forgotten truth re-sprung.

¶

The truth-seeker's battle goes on day and night; as long as life lasts, it never ceases.

¶

It is not enough to avoid speaking a lie. One must not hear it or love it.

¶

If you have faith, you can believe a common piece of stone to be a god; otherwise, it is nothing but a stone.

¶

Keep seven cubits away from a horse and fourteen from a drunkard, but as far as you can from a bastard.

¶

The grass suffers in the fight of the tiger and the buffalo.

¶

To the mediocre, mediocrity appears great.

¶

In the friendship of asses, look out for kicks.

¶

Neither too much talk nor too great a silence, neither continuous rain nor continuous sunshine, is desirable. But while the weather is not at your command, your tongue is.

¶

Fate and self-help share equally in shaping our destiny.

¶

It is easy for the shopkeeper to promise full weight when he has not agreed to sell.

¶

Men grind a knife because they dislike it blunt, but when they have sharpened it, it cuts their fingers. In similar manner, men seek wealth because they dislike poverty, but when they amass it, they often find it brings them pain.

¶

What is impertinence? When the jackal is born in August and there is a flood in September and the jackal pup says, "Good gracious! I never saw such a high flood!"

¶

At least the ambitious man dies for fame. The glutton dies but for his belly.

¶

The crow is capable of learning the walk of the goose. But, in doing so, it loses its own.

¶

Do not trouble to preserve your hair if you plan to cut off your head.

¶

The cricket mounted on a bundle of twigs says, "I am the owner of all this wealth." His position lasts until the first jolt.

¶

A thirsty man must go to the well. For the well will never come to him.

¶

The way to overcome the angry man is with gentleness; the evil man with goodness; the miser with generosity; and the liar with truth.

¶

The best remedies are found by those who suffer.

¶

One works on his own salvation by serving his fellow man.

¶

It is ironical that age slows one down. For the older one grows, the more eager is he to work fast, lest time run out.

¶

It is the *spirit* of the quest which determines its outcome.

¶

The truly great man seeks not gain. Neither does he indulge himself in despising those who do.

¶

To be eclipsed by someone need not destroy you. The sunshine seems all the brighter when the moon's shadow has passed away.

¶

A man without morals is like a letter without a stamp
—it will go nowhere.

¶

And when your life's tale is finished, who will be the
hero?

FROM CHINA

Sometimes, to deviate an inch is to lose a thousand
miles.

¶

Though man cannot reach perfection in a hundred
years, he can fall in a day with time to spare.

¶

It is better to go than send.

¶

Scholars are their country's treasure and the richest ornaments of the feast.

¶

Would you know politics, read history.

¶

Just scales and full measure injure no man.

¶

It is worthier to do a kindness at home than to go far in order to burn incense.

¶

One generation plants the trees; another sits in their shade.

¶

Unskilled fools quarrel with their tools.

¶

As meat is the cure of hunger, so is study the cure of ignorance.

¶

In enacting laws, rigor is indispensable; in executing them, mercy.

¶

If you suspect a man, don't employ him; if you employ a man, don't suspect him.

¶

Gold has its price. Learning is priceless.

¶

If you travel by boat, be prepared for a ducking.

¶

A whitewashed crow will not remain white for long.

¶

One dog barks at something and a hundred bark at the sound.

¶

He that takes medicine and neglects diet, wastes the skill of the physician.

¶

Rats know the way of rats.

¶

The best cure for drunkeness is, whilst sober, to observe a drunken man.

¶

A people without faith in themselves cannot survive.

¶

If you don't want anyone to know it, don't do it.

¶

It is too late to pull the rein when the horse has gained the brink of the precipice.

¶

If a man does not receive guests at home, he will meet with very few hosts abroad.

¶

It is easier to govern a kingdom than to rule one's family.

¶

To rise early three mornings is to gain a day of time.

¶

Think not any vice trivial and so practice it; think not any virtue trivial, and so neglect it.

¶

The mind can make a heaven of hell, a hell of heaven.

¶

If you continually grind a bar of iron, you will eventually make a needle of it.

¶

It is difficult to satisfy one's appetite by painting pictures of cakes.

¶

Examine the neighborhood before you choose your house.

¶

The tongue is like a sharp knife. It can kill without drawing blood.

¶

It is easier to visit friends than to live with them.

¶

If good luck comes, who doesn't?
If good luck does not come, who does?

¶

The best way to avoid punishment is to fear it.

¶

To know the truth is easy; but oh! how difficult to follow it!

¶

It is easy to go from economy to extravagance. It is hard to go from extravagance to economy.

¶

Preserve the old but know the new.

¶

A cat is as brave as a lion—behind his own door.

¶

If you wish to know everything about a man's mind, listen to his words.

¶

Falling hurts least those who fly low.

¶

Should you wish to know the road through the mountains, ask those who have already trodden it.

¶

Tigers and deer do not stroll together. The crow does not roost with the phoenix. So, too, is a man known by his friends.

¶

It is the beautiful bird that gets caged.

¶

The Great Wall stands; the builder is gone.

¶

A thief is a thief whether he steals a diamond or a cucumber.

¶

The tail of China is large and will not be wagged.

¶

And from Chairman Mao Tse-tung's *Little Red Book* . . .

"It is well known that when you do anything, unless you understand its actual circumstances, its nature and its relations to other things, you will not know the laws governing it, or know how to do it, or be able to do it well."

¶

"Even if we achieve gigantic successes in our work, there is no reason whatsoever to feel conceited and arrogant. Modesty helps one to go forward, whereas conceit makes one lag behind. This is a truth we must always bear in mind."

¶

"We must learn to look at problems all-sidedly, seeing the reverse as well as the obverse side of things. In given conditions, a bad thing can lead to good results and a good thing to bad results."

CLOSINGS

getting off while
you're still ahead

A long-winded speaker was once interrupted by a member of his audience, who shouted "Enough! Enough! I don't agree! Let me answer you!" To which the speaker retorted, quickly enough: "You may speak for the present generation, sir, but I speak for posterity." "Yes," countered the man in the audience, "and it seems you are determined to speak until your constituency arrives!"

The single most often-committed crime against audiences is that of speaking too long. No matter that a man is brilliant; if he is also long in the tongue, his brilliance is bound to lose some of its shine. And, of course, there is nothing as painful as a speaker with only a couple of things to say—who doesn't stop when he's already said them.

On the other hand, a good speech, delivered with snap and variety, with changes of pace and good humor, can make a platform hero of even an ordinary man—provided he knows when to get off!

The best time to get off is when you've said all you need say (but not all you *could* say) to make your points. Then, when you're still ahead, wind up with a line, an anecdote, a proverb, a quote, or some other memorable piece of copy that leaves your audience laughing, or thoughtful—depending upon the subject of your address.

One of the great advantages of ending with a laugh —and this can be done even with serious speeches by using stories or fables that reaffirm your main point cleverly, rather than repetitiously—is that the laughter and applause you'll win from your audience as you sit down gives the impression that you are being applauded for your entire speech. And what happens during your last few seconds on the platform will have a strong bearing on what they will take away with them when it's all over.

So, if you want to go away popular, appreciated, and applauded, leave 'em laughing. If this isn't possible, if the occasion is such that humor is totally out of place, then leave 'em with the best line or paragraph in your speech —some brilliantly phrased comment that will make them cheer you for your sensitivity and depth.

This chapter on closings offers you some proven-successful ways to end a talk. But you might find the right closing for your speech *anywhere* in this book. Every chapter offers possibilities. Be sure to go through it again, page by page, scanning the material for a suitable thought with which to make your exit. There are some fine possibilities in the chapter on Fables and in The 10 Best Speech Bits. Many superb exit lines are to be found in the chapter on Proverbs. And, of course, use the Subject Index if you're seeking closing material on a specific topic.

It may seem to you that the amount of time spent in selecting the right closing is out of proportion to the time you've spent on the entire talk. Not so. Those final words are of such importance that no amount of time devoted to finding them is too much. Remember: all the work, all the research, all the worrying, all the pruning and editing and rehearsing that have gone into preparing for your appearance on the platform will pay off for you during that single moment when you make your exit amidst the cheers, the whistling, the laughter, and that burst of final applause.

¶

Well, I have been talking for quite a while, and I would now like to throw in a bit of statistical information. I don't know if you know this, but it has been estimated that the average man speaks 25,000 words a day, and the average woman, 30,000. Unfortunately, when I come home each day, I've already spoken my 25,000—and my wife hasn't started her 30,000.

Up here on the platform, I have used up a week's words. And, lest I be forced to listen to my wife without interruption for the next month, I think I had better come to an end.

¶

In conclusion, I would like to offer you a quotation from Louis D. Brandeis. Said Mr. Brandeis: "Nine tenths of the serious controversies which arise in life result from misunderstanding, result from one man not knowing the facts which to the other man seem important, or otherwise failing to appreciate his point of view."

I have attempted today to present some of the facts that seem important to me, to give you my point of view. If, in examining these facts and viewpoints, we can be brought a bit closer to the solution of our mutual problems, then my appearance here today will have been worthwhile.

> The Brandeis quote could be followed by any number of concluding statements. The one given here is merely a for-instance.

¶

Well, it was nice being here with a group of such extinguished-looking gentlemen.

¶

A quote in closing that urges some stock-
taking about the way we have been creating ecological problems:

"We human beings are rushing forward unthinkingly
through days of incredible accomplishments, of glory
and of tragedy, our eyes seeking the stars—or fixed too
often upon each other in hatred and conflict. We have
forgotten the earth, forgotten it in the sense that we
fail to regard it as the source of our life."
[HENRY FAIRFIELD OSBORN]

¶

Calvin Coolidge once was known to remark that "If
you don't say anything, you won't be called upon to
repeat it."

Well, I cannot be sure whether I have uttered any
thoughts that will bear repeating—but I certainly hope
that I have.

¶

"The 'great' commitment all too easily obscures the
'little' one. But without the humility and warmth

which you have to develop . . . to the few with whom you are personally involved, you will never be able to do anything for the many. Love . . . would remain powerless against the negative forces within you, if it were not tamed by the yoke of human intimacy and warmed by its tenderness." [DAG HAMMARSKJÖLD]

¶

I have talked a good deal up here about change. But I fully realize that change is not as easy to accept as one might think. Most people have something of the attitude of the lady who attended a lecture in New Orleans where Wernher Von Braun was talking on the subject of putting a man on the moon. When his lecture was over, he made the mistake that most speakers make—he asked if there were any questions.

A woman's hand shot up, and Dr. Von Braun called on her for her question.

"Why," asked the woman, "can't you forget about getting people on the moon, and stay home and watch television like the good Lord intended for you to do?"

¶

Our speeches are over, and now we will ask you to fill out the papers [or questionnaires] you have been given. Please keep this in mind: legibility is a virtue! And profanity will be accepted only if it has artistic merit or redeeming social value.

¶

This quote, from H. G. Barnett's book *Innovation*, gives you a thought-provoking way to come to a concluding note in your talk if you have presented new or innovative ideas, or if you are asking your audience to entertain some:

"Innovation is the linkage or fusion of two or more elements that have not been previously joined in this fashion, so that the result is a qualitatively distinct whole. It's like a genetic cross or hybrid: it is totally different from either of its parents, but it resembles both of them in some respects."

¶

I think I had better conclude, before I become like the speaker who appeared on a program where Will Rogers was the moderator. This speaker had continued well beyond his allotted time, and when he finally sat down, Will Rogers arose and said: "You have just heard from that famous Chinese orator, *On Too-long.*"

¶

On a plane bound for Europe, the pilot's voice
suddenly came over the public address system:

"Ladies and gentlemen," the pilot said, "I have
two pieces of news for you. One of them is good, and
one of them is not so good. So I'll tell you the bad
news first. The bad news is that we are lost—we don't
have any idea of where we are. But, as I told you,
there's good news, too. The good news is that we have
a 200-mile-an-hour tail wind."

From this story, you can bridge into some
final comments in which you state that
there are times when it seems that the
story sums up the current state of American society (or of universities, or of youth,
or of Congress, etc.): we don't know
where we are going, but, quite clearly, we
are getting there awfully fast.

¶

"Our main business is not to see what lies dimly at a
distance, but to do what lies clearly at hand."
[THOMAS CARLYLE]

¶

I have taken a good deal of your time here today. Hopefully, you have had it to spare. And what is "time" really for? Let me answer my own question by quoting Max Kaplan, the author of *Leisure in America*.

Mr. Kaplan writes: "The average middle-class home in America has in it enough vacuum cleaners, dishwashers, clothes scrubbers, and other gadgets to equal the energy of ninety male servants. This 'supplements' time, providing the American style of life."

"In addition," continues Mr. Kaplan, "we have at our disposal better lights, frozen foods, telephones in all colors, unpaid-for cars, paper-covered books, and countless other paraphernalia that *enrich* time, helping us to *save* it, *pass* it, *spend* it, *kill* it, or *use* it for a variety of purposes."

¶

I hope I have made some small contribution to the subject under discussion today, particularly since it is the only area in which I enjoy any sort of expertise at all. There are so many other subjects about which I know absolutely nothing—like sports. I know so little about sports that, when they asked me what I thought of the Indianapolis 500, I said I thought they were all guilty.

> If you happen to be on a program where some sports figure is also scheduled to speak, or to be introduced, you can use the above bit with a different lead in: "I'm amazed that I'm even in the same room with a prominent sports figure. I know so little about sports . . ."

¶

A southern minister whose sermon had developed the point that salvation is free—free as the water we drink —was then obliged to complain that the collection was scandalously small that day. A member of the congregation rose up to remind the minister that he had said salvation was as free as water.

"Indeed it is," replied the minister, "but when we pipe it to you, you have to pay for the plumbing."

> The above material can be used if you are a speaker who must end by asking your audience for something—money, pledges, signatures on a petition, action, etc.

¶

You have been a fine and attentive audience, and I thank you for it and hope it has been worth your while. As Wilson Mizner once said, "A good listener is not only popular everywhere, but after a while he knows something."

¶

In concluding, I would like to borrow from John W. Gardner's book, *Excellence*. Gardner tells us that "Mankind is not divided into two categories, those who are creative and those who are not. There are degrees of the attribute. It is the rare individual who has it in his power to achieve the highest reaches of creativity. But many could achieve fairly impressive levels of creativity under favorable circumstances. And quite a high proportion of the population could show some creativity some of the time, in some aspect of their lives."

In describing further the characteristics of the creative person, Gardner goes on to say that "Unlike the rest of us, he does not persist stubbornly and unproductively in one approach to a problem."

Why have I read these excerpts? Because it is going to take creativity to solve the problems we have been discussing here today. And it is my opinion that this audience is made up of enough people who, in one degree or another, can lend various aspects of their creativity to finding and executing solutions.

¶

When John D. Rockefeller III, was chairman of the Board of Trustees of the Population Council, he said something in a speech I was privileged to hear that sums up my final thought, and I can do no better than to quote him directly:

"Man is more than animal. He has mental, emotional and spiritual needs that go far beyond bare necessities, creature comforts and material resources. Every man deserves at least the chance to lead a life of satisfaction and purpose, to achieve in life more than mere existence.

"Even if science by some magic could show the way to feed new billions of people, we still would not have solved the population problem. The *quality* of life cannot be omitted from the solution. Indeed, there can be no true solution until society can offer every individual an opportunity—in the fullest sense—to live as well as to survive."

¶

When a speaker says, "Well, to make a long story short," it's too late.

I hope we have not arrived at a point where it is already too late. For I have just about come to my conclusions.

¶

It has been my job to speak, and yours to listen. I do hope we finished at the same time.

¶

In the late nineteenth century, a famous man wrote these words: "If we would only testify to the truth as we see it, it would turn out at once that there are hundreds, thousands, even millions of men just as we are, who see the truth as we do, are afraid, as we are, of seeming to be singular by confessing it, and are only waiting, again as we are, for someone to proclaim it."

The man who wrote that was Leo Tolstoi.

As Americans, we may not agree with other theories and ideas of that famous Russian; but I, for one, cannot help but agree with those words. And I

have attempted today to "testify to the truth," as I
see it.

¶

I have presented many facts in my talk, and I would
like, if you will bear with me, to draw some
conclusions from these facts. For even with all the facts
at hand, it is possible for people to come to different—
and sometimes erroneous—conclusions.

It's rather like the Eskimo who went on a visit for
the first time to New York. When he came back to
Eskimo land, he had a long, narrow package, wrapped
in gift paper and tied with a big ribbon. His wife asked
him what it was, and he told her it was a present for
her. She opened it, and inside was a long length of
pipe. She thanked him and then asked him again, "But
what is it?"

"It's a great invention," he said. "They use it in
New York. You prop it upright in the bedroom, one
end on the floor, and the other end at the ceiling.
When you have a very cold night, you rap on it and
you get heat."

¶

It has been said that a good orator implies a good audience.

From where I stand, you have been a fine audience indeed. And if you have found my oration to be good, then that, too, is a credit to all of you out front.

¶

"I have talked a good deal about creativity and I want to make one final point—absolving myself from any impression you may have gained that I think I can make creativity happen. I cannot, and anyone who tells you he can is kidding himself. I think creativity can easily be managed to death. On the other hand, it can also be starved to death—or worked to death. The most valuable contribution that a good manager can make is to create an environment in which creativity can flourish without being managed, starved, or worked to death."   [STEPHEN O. FRANKFURT]

¶

Permit me to end with a passage from William Saroyan:

"What can a man do to move along in some kind of grace through his days and years? Well, there are a million ways of putting it, but it always comes to pretty much the one way—he can do his best, in accordance with his laws, and in keeping with his truth, in favor of himself, and on behalf of his expectation to see it all through in the best possible style, with some meaning, and without harm to anybody else."

¶

Samuel Johnson was discussing with one of his students a report he had just given. Mr. Johnson told the student: "I found your speech to be good—and original. However, the part that was good was not original. And the part that was original, was not good."

I hope you will not go away saying the same about my talk.

¶

Since this audience is made up of people from many countries, it is possible that my remarks have hit each of you somewhat differently. For there is, certainly, a difference in the way people in various parts of the world see things. I once read a book called *The Rich Man's Guide to Europe* in which the author, one Charles Graves, explains such differences this way:

"The Danes are great jokers; they love a laugh. It was a Dane who invented the story of an International Congress of Zoologists who were requested to prepare a thesis on elephants. Most people remember that the American contribution was 'How to Raise Bigger and Better Elephants.' The British contributed 'On Safari Through Darkest Africa,' which was subtitled 'Preparation of Tea for Elephants.' The French contribution was 'Les Amours de l'Eléphant,' while the Germans came up with 'A Cursory Introduction to the Biology of Elephants' (in fourteen volumes). The Scandinavian variants may be less well known. The Swedish version was 'What Title to Use in Addressing Elephants,' the Norwegian one was 'Norway and the Norwegians,' and the Danish, 'One Hundred Ways to Prepare Elephants for the Cold Table.' "

Despite the possibility of varying interpretations, let me nonetheless state my conclusions.

¶

In talking about life under the sea, an oceanographer once commented that it was one thing to glimpse a new world and quite another to establish permanent outposts in it and work and live in it. The same might be said about our explorations of the moon.

But, much closer to home, we can say the same about the difference between theory and application. I have offered you my theories. I do not for a minute suggest that their applications will be quite so simple to come by.

¶

In the year 50 B.C., someone inscribed upon an ancient wall these words: "Conversation is the image of the mind. As the mind is, so is the talk."

In my talk today, I have tried to reveal—not hide —what is on my mind. I know that my words will not, like the quote I just gave you, live two thousand years. But if they give you food for thought, then I will be satisfied.

¶

Well, I have been going on and on for quite a bit, and I imagine you are all anxious to go eat. So I will end by telling you a remark I heard last Saturday night at a swinging party I went to. A couple I know had been hoisting the martinis rather steadily for quite some time. Finally, I heard the lady say to her mate, "Honey, you'd better stop drinking. Your face is getting awfully blurred."

I'm afraid your faces are also getting a bit blurred, so I had better knock it off. Thank you for your kind attention, and for the invitation to address you.

¶

Mark Twain once said that between himself and Rudyard Kipling he felt—and I quote—"We have all the knowledge in the world."

Perhaps the last speaker and I gave the impression of having all the knowledge in the world, on both sides of the question; but I assure you that such is not the case. In fact, we will now throw the floor open to discussion, so that you can learn firsthand how much knowledge we lack.

¶

Well, as an old Texas friend of mine used to say: "If you haven't struck oil in the first half hour, stop *boring.*"

¶

If nothing else, the speeches here today have pointed up how many problems we have and how much unhappiness accompanies these problems. Which is sad. For, as Archibald MacLeish once said, "We have more in our garages and kitchens and cellars today than Louis XIV had in the whole of Versailles!"

¶

Of course, you may not agree with my diagnosis as I have expounded on it up here. They are currently telling the story of the three scientists who were working with some highly dangerous radioactive material when a big explosion occurred in their laboratory. The three doctors were examined by the company physician, who looked very grave and said: "Gentlemen, I have bad news. Each of you has but two months to live. But since the accident happened on company time, the company is willing to grant whatever last wishes you may have for the end of your lives."

The first scientist was an Englishman, and he thought seriously for a few minutes and then said: "I rather imagine I would like to spend the end of my days back in old England. I shall just sit in my club and read the London *Times* and talk politics with my chums."

The second scientist was a Russian, and he told the doctor: "My family lives on the outskirts of Leningrad, and I would like to be with them, sharing the community pleasures, visiting the Hermitage when I can, and enjoying party lectures on the radio."

The doctor then turned to the third man, who was an old Jewish scientist, and asked him for *his* last wish. "Well," replied the third scientist, "to tell you the truth, I'd like to get a second opinion from another doctor."

You are, naturally, free to look for other opinions.

¶

I once heard something attributed to Frank Lloyd Wright. "Early in life," he is reputed to have said, "I had to choose between honest arrogance and hypocritical humility. I chose honest arrogance and have seen no occasion to change."

I didn't have to make that choice early in life. But in preparing my opinions for presentation here today, it was a choice I had to come to grips with. Like Frank Lloyd Wright, I chose honest arrogance—as I imagine you detected in my remarks—and I hope you will find it in your hearts to forgive me for it.

¶

I may not have come off as being very tactful in my remarks. But I share the feelings of Sir Frank Medlicott, an English solicitor who once made this statement: "Some people mistake weakness for tact. If they are silent when they ought to speak and so feign an agreement they do not feel, they call it being tactful. Cowardice would be a much better name. Tact is an active quality that is not exercised by merely making a dash for cover. Be sure, when you think you are being extremely tactful, that you are not in reality running away from something you ought to face."

I have done my best to face the facts as I see them . . .

¶

During the course of this meeting, we have heard a great deal about what is new in our field. The fact that there is so much which *is* new reminded me of something I once read that the physicist Robert Oppenheimer said: "One thing that is new is the prevalence of newness, the changing scale and scope of change itself, so that the world alters as we walk in it, so that the years of man's life measure not some small growth or rearrangement or moderation of what he learned in childhood, but a great upheaval."

I, too, feel that what we are experiencing is, indeed, a great upheaval.

¶

We have covered a lot of territory here today; but then, we appear to be headed for a time in history when we may all end up like the man who refused to become a specialist because there were so many wonderful things to know about in our great bustling world.

"I am a generalist," he said, "and my purpose is to know less and less about more and more, until I know absolutely nothing about absolutely everything."

¶

Let me read you a quotation. It is from a man named John Jay Chapman: "So long as there is any subject which men may not freely discuss, they are timid upon *all* subjects. They wear an iron crown and talk in whispers."

We have not spoken here today in whispers. We have talked freely, which may leave us open to outside criticism. But I would rather have that than wear an iron crown.

¶

I have now come to a point where I want to tell you something I was once taught, although the lesson is something I have a tendency to forget. I was taught that the four most important words in our language are "What is your opinion?", that the three most important words are "If you please," the two most important ones are "Thank you," and the single most important word is "you." I was also taught that the *least* important word is "I."

I—if I may once again use an unimportant one— have not adhered closely to this belief, having tortured the word "I" perhaps needlessly. But now, in opening the meeting to a discussion from the floor, I want to ask, "If you please, what is your opinion?" to hear what *you* have to say—and, finally, to say "Thank you."

¶

I will remind you about the story of a Boy Scout who showed up at his troop meeting with a black eye. When his scoutmaster asked him what had happened, he replied that he had tried to help a little old lady across the street. "How in the world," asked the scoutmaster, "could you get a black eye doing that?" To which the scout replied, "She didn't want to go."

I am a bit like the Boy Scout. I have been trying— not too subtly, I fear—to lead you across the street. And I have detected a bit of resistance to going. However, even if we have come halfway together, I will be pleased.

¶

In closing, I would like to tell you something that Pierre Curie, the Nobel Prize-winning chemist, once said. "Humanity," said Monsieur Curie, "surely needs practical men who make the best of their work for their own interest, without forgetting the general interest. But it needs also dreamers, for whom the unselfish following of a purpose is so imperative that it becomes impossible for them to devote much attention to their own material benefit."

Perhaps the ideas I have expressed up here today have not been in the realm of practicality. But I hope that I have set some of you to dreaming—and that you will find your dreams so imperative as to want to make of them a lifetime goal.

¶

In conclusion, I would like to point out something that John W. Gardner, the head of Common Cause, has stated so beautifully. "We must never forget," said Mr. Gardner, "that though the word may be popular, the consequences of true creativity can never be assured of popularity. New ways threaten the old, and those who are wedded to the old may prove highly intolerant. Our affection is generally reserved for innovators long dead."

¶

I once heard that someone had written a book called *An Unbiased Opinion of the Civil War, from a Southern Point of View.*

I fear that my own comments up here today have been equally unbiased.

¶

There are places in this world where my remarks might be misunderstood—not because others lack in understanding, but because our ways are not always the ways of others. Much of what we think and do would prove curious in other lands. Americans don't always recognize this.

For example, Donald Swann, the actor, tells about the Indian man he sat next to on a flight from Fiji to Calcutta, who was completely baffled by the breakfast served on their Pan Am jet. First, he poured his coffee into the cornflakes and ate them. Then he mixed the milk and the sugar and drank it. Next, he licked the butter from the small square of paper. And for a chaser, he drank the marmalade.

¶

"Everything has an end—except a sausage, which has two." So goes an old Danish proverb. Well, this talk is not a sausage, although it may have seemed hammy in certain spots. So it has come, at last, to its end.

¶

You may recall the year when Hubert Humphrey was running for the Presidency against Richard Nixon. You may also recall that Mr. Humphrey, in conversation or on the platform, was not known particularly for his brevity. In fact, it was reported at that time that Muriel Humphrey once said to her husband, "Hubert— a speech doesn't have to be eternal to be immortal."

I will keep that in mind and come to some very quick conclusions.

¶

The best speeches are those that have good beginnings and good endings—close together.

MAKING LOVE TO YOUR VISUALS

so that they work
harder for you

I was once conducting a course for business executives who wanted to improve their public speaking techniques as well as their ability to make presentations in front of sizeable groups of people. One evening, I had invited my good friend José Quintero, the famous Broadway director who won the Pulitzer Prize for his brilliant direction of Eugene O'Neill's *Long Day's Journey into Night*, to appear as our guest lecturer.

The subject of the session was "The Use of Visuals," and I launched the program by asking Mr. Quintero how a speaker could make the most of them. "I can tell you," he replied, "in five words: *Make love to your visuals!*"

Mr. Quintero then demonstrated what he meant. As though holding on to something precious, he put his arm firmly around a stack of cards that rested on an easel beside him. Then he drew the audience's attention to the waiting visuals by quietly announcing that he was "about to reveal some dramatic and telling facts." He paused to let this sink in; and as he took his arm from the cards, he carefully straightened them—almost lovingly. By now, all eyes were glued to the easel. Slowly, he removed the cover card, revealing his first visual. Without any rush at all, he read off the headline, lending emphasis to each word by gently tapping it with his index finger. Before continuing with the remainder of the material on that card, he moved in front of the easel, completely hiding the visual material from the audience, and repeated the headline. Only then did he move aside and permit the audience to see what the balance of the card contained.

What a difference from the average speaker, who rattles off the words on his visual aids—often in a mumble that communicates his own disinterest in the message— finally casting each card aside as though glad to be rid of it!

If the nature and subject matter of your talk suggest a need for visual material, you'll want to be sure that you're using it in a way that will enhance and enforce your message. All too often, even capable speakers do themselves a disservice by hiding behind their props and using them as crutches. Many speakers seem unaware that their visuals are not truly helping them, but are actually fighting the spoken message.

The advice in this chapter is based upon more than five hundred separate experiences in using visuals with speeches and presentations of various types—presentations designed to convince an audience of a point of view, to rebut an opposing viewpoint, to make a sale, to get agreement for action on a proposal, to describe an experience or an accomplishment, to teach, to preach, or to entertain. The suggestions cover such visuals as can be designed in advance of the presentation, not drawings or blackboard demonstrations which are created right before the eyes of the audience—although even such on-the-spot visual aids can benefit from some of the techniques described here.

DECIDING WHAT TYPES OF VISUALS TO USE may be the most important decision you'll have to make regarding this aspect of your presentation. The easiest way out for too many speakers is to settle for a slide presentation. I say easy because the slides will be shown in a darkened or semi-darkened room (permitting the speaker to "hide"), on a screen that is physically out of reach of the podium ("You see, they're not really related to me!"). The speaker need only turn his script over to a visualizer and say, "Make me some slides," and when they arrive in their neat little frames, a *fait accompli*, no one will deny that they look professional and unassailable.

All of these factors help to (1) separate the presenter from his audience; (2) impersonalize the presentation; and (3) give the audience a chance to doze. Unless you are an unusually gifted speaker or have a message of gut concern to the audience, the turning off of the lights before the slides go on is tacit permission to the listener to turn off his cortex.

NEVER USE SLIDES UNLESS THE AUDIENCE IS SO LARGE IT COULDN'T SEE A MORE INTIMATE VISUAL AID. You may

properly ask, "How large is 'too large'?" I have used 40"
× 50" charts before an audience of forty people and,
because the charts were designed with the size of the
audience in mind, everyone in the room could see everything. Of course, the seating arrangements in your auditorium or conference room will also determine how good
the visibility will be. In a theater-type room where the
seats are fixed in place, whether or not a group of forty
persons can see your "live" visuals will depend on how far
apart the rows are and whether one row of heads will
block another, as well as on the size of the lettering and
pictures on your cards. (If you have a choice, avoid such
a theater arrangement for forty people or fewer.) If you
can arrange for a long conference table—or better yet,
two or three tables with chairs clustered around them—
you can easily place this number of people so that they
can see your charts. With less than forty, *never* put your
audience in the dark, and never mechanize your visuals.
If your audience is a large one and you have no alternative
but to use slides, there are ways to avoid the pitfalls of
darkness—I'll tell you about them later on. Of course,
motion picture film, since it moves and sometimes talks or
has a sound track, is the exception; it is another matter
entirely. For reasons that you can guess, a good motion
film provides an excellent change of pace and can actually
wake up a sluggish audience. But most speakers have
neither the money nor the time to create, or have someone create for them, a motion picture film that can be
used to strengthen their talk. (There are, of course, excep-
tions. For example, campus recruiters for large companies

are often supplied with short films to supplement their oral presentations.)

IF YOU USE PRESENTATION CARDS OR FLIP CHARTS, DON'T LET THEM FIGHT YOU. A visual of any kind is supposed to help you get across your message. If it fails to do that, it has no reason for being. Visuals also often serve as props for the speaker, serving to remind him of points he wishes to make if he is not reading a complete script. There is nothing wrong with this, *provided it does not become the sole purpose of the visual.*

Here are some thoughts to keep in mind when designing and producing your presentation cards or charts:

YOUR VISUAL MUST REINFORCE YOUR MESSAGE BY ADDING TO IT OR MAKING IT MORE MEMORABLE. If the visual is saying one thing while you are saying another, one of you is going to lose out. It just isn't possible for the audience to think two different things at the same moment, so whichever has a stronger appeal—your voice or the material on the card—will win. Usually the visual wins, so it's best to avoid this kind of infighting by putting nothing on your visual aid that will take the audience away from you.

Let me give you an example. Suppose that you are giving a speech to two dozen students about to be graduated from college, and your talk is designed to get these people to consider joining the Peace Corps. You have just made this statement: "It is not only what you can do in the Peace Corps, but what the Peace Corps can do for you." If you are using visuals in this presentation, and if they are wholly, or partially, in the form of flip cards, you might go on to say: "Let's examine both aspects of that statement." Perhaps you will want to use two cards to help your audience follow, *and remember*, the arguments you wish to present. One card might be headlined YOU AND THE PEACE CORPS; the second card, THE PEACE CORPS AND YOU. On the first of these cards, under your heading, these key words might appear:

1. Teach your speciality
2. Encourage self-help
3. Improve standard of living
4. Promote independence
5. Make friends for U. S. A.

On the second card, perhaps these points are lettered:

1. Develop independence—*yours*
2. Improve problem-solving abilities
3. Discover your strengths
4. Discover your weaknesses
5. Experience true friendship and love

Since these are only key words designed to help the audience retain most or all of the ten points on the two cards, you will no doubt amplify each item in your speech. If such amplification is brief, you can afford to have the five points on a single card. But audiences have a tendency to leave the speaker and read ahead—so if you're going to spend several minutes on each idea, you would be well-advised to list only a single point on a card and use a total of ten cards to make these points. Perhaps each point could be illustrated with a suitable drawing or photograph.

Still another device would be to have each lettered item covered with a thin, but opaque, piece of paper, which you could rip off each item as you get ready to talk about it. This helps maintain suspense and interest in what is about to come. It also creates an automatic summary of each group of five points when all the covering papers have been removed.

WHAT ARE THE PITFALLS IN CREATING SUCH VISUALS? There are three major mistakes that are commonly made in designing flip cards (or, for that matter, slides) such as the ones just described. First, there is the tendency to letter complete sentences, even paragraphs—which provides the speaker with a talking script, but which alienates the audience from him. For one thing, if you put too much copy on a card the lettering is bound to be small, and your audience is less likely to be able to make out the words. Then, if your audience is reading the sentences or paragraphs, they're not listening to you *unless you're saying precisely the same words.* In which case, if everything is being said in writing, who needs *you?* Why not just send your cards? On the other hand, if the cards carry sentences and you choose to speak different sentences (thus giving the impression that you are not dependent upon your aids), you're creating confusion in the mind of the listener-viewer. *So use only key words!*

What are the other pitfalls? The second is the tendency to let an art director run away with himself and over-design the visual aid, so that the "designy" aspects— the multicolors or the fancy lettering—serve to detract from the message. A visual aid should not be a test of the artist's decorating talents; *it is a test of his ability to communicate visually*. This doesn't mean that you shouldn't use color in your flip charts. On the contrary, there is no reason to limit yourself to black, or to a single color, provided the color that is used is used to help get the message across and not to work against it. *Just be certain each card doesn't become a circus poster.*

The third danger that visual designers sometimes subject their cards to is illegibility. Fancy script, tiny type, too little space between lines of copy, reverse type (white lettering on black or colored background)—all these tend to make copy on a card or chart inaccessible to the viewer. Nothing is more frustrating than to have a speaker say, "As you can see from these figures . . ." and for the audience not to be able to see at all, because everything has been designed for close-up reading and not for audience absorption. The more the people in the audience have to strain to see, the less they're going to concentrate on what you're saying. And when they discover that they really can't see anything, they usually give up trying. When they do that, they may also give up listening.

VISUALS SHOULD BE ALIVE—OTHERWISE, THEY'RE DEADLY. If it's necessary for you to use a large number of visuals (whether they are flip cards or slides), their sameness—if they all follow a single format and are unrelieved by illustration or proper use of color—can act as a soporific. There are a number of ways to make your visuals more interesting without letting them take over. Sometimes you can introduce a visual *theme* in the form of color or illustration.

A *color theme* would work this way: assuming you have eight ideas to present and, within these, there are a number of other subfactors to visualize, you can assign a color to each of the eight ideas—red, green, blue, orange, purple, yellow, brown, and magenta. Each idea (or each "section") would then utilize only the color assigned to it, plus the color of the lettering—probably black or sepia. Headline copy, illustrations, or perhaps just the underlining of the headlines would use this assigned color. When the next idea is presented, the audience knows immediately that it is to shift gears because the color has changed. At the end, if the eight points are to be summarized, the summary might be done in all eight colors; or, if this is too gaudy because there is too much copy, each of the eight numbers which precede the summary lines could pick up the previously used color. Color can also enhance your visuals if you use it only for *illustrations*. In such cases, the lettering could then be in black, sepia, or some other legible color.

Another way to make your visuals come alive is to use only pictures—perhaps photographs, if available—and let the speech do the talking while the pictures reinforce your words. For example, if you were giving a talk to raise funds for war orphans, your text might call for you to say: "Last year, 10,000 of these children under the age of five died of protein deficiency." As you said the words "these children," you would flip your chart to reveal a blowup of a war orphan clearly suffering from malnutrition.

Still another device which can successfully enliven your visuals, particularly if you must show a large number of graphs or statistical information, is to humanize your statistics by turning them into "things," or people. Let's say you want to tell your audience that the consumption of pickles in this country has increased steadily during the last decade. Instead of using a graph that employs lines and numbers, show a small mound of pickles for the year of lowest consumption; more and more pickles for the years when the consumption increases; and, finally, pickles tumbling off the chart for the year of maximum consumption. If you are talking about people instead of pickles, you might use stick figures or heads. If you are talking about housing construction, then you'd want to use small houses, or roofs with TV antennas, or some other symbol of a home that would appeal to your particular audience.

IF YOU HAVE TO USE SLIDES, THEY HAVE TO BE GOOD. When using flip cards, you can quickly sense whether the audience is paying attention to them. If interest lags at any point, you can then make a quick decision to skip a section of the cards and cover that material verbally only. You can interrupt the use of cards by walking in front of your easel and expanding on some point without any visual assistance. Or you can even break into your own presentation with some ad lib designed to elicit audience response, such as: "You know, I had a very talented young man assigned to work out these visuals—I'm sure he had every reason to be a bit on the arrogant side. Sometimes, however, he carried it a little far. One morning I stopped by to see how my charts were progressing and, as I entered his office, I said, "Beautiful morning!" to which he replied, "Thank you!"

But once the lights are dimmed and your *slides* begin to flash on the screen, you are enslaved by them. This is particularly so if the slides are being flashed by a projectionist in a booth and he changes slides in accordance with the copy on your script, as prearranged during rehearsal. They simply have to be right, and they have to be good.

There are certain things you can do to insure a successful presentation with slides. Some of these are mentioned above with respect to flip cards and charts. They include: making sure that everything you want the audience to read is legible; proper use of color, so that it lends variety but does not take over; working to have each visual reinforce your message, not fight it; using key words only, and avoiding body copy; and "humanizing" your graphs and statistics. All of these suggestions apply equally to slides.

But there is another bit of advice dictated by experience. If you use slides, group them together so that they are all used in one segment of your talk and not scattered throughout the presentation. If you use one slide here, a couple there, then you're literally keeping your audience in the dark even during those sections of the speech when no visuals are in use. On the other hand, if you use all of your slides during a single segment of your presentation, they can actually give you a good change of pace. Then, when the lights go on again and the focus of attention returns to you, you will be speaking to an audience that has just had its interest renewed by the introduction of something new in the proceedings.

Another way to make the slide portion of your talk heighten interest, rather than decrease it, is to use a larger number of slides *within any given slide period*, and have them flashed onto the screen more rapidly. My rule of thumb is to aim for fifteen seconds or less for each slide. I realize that this is not always possible. If there is statistical information to be presented against a particular slide ("This slide shows you how our corporation spent its gross income last year"), and if it takes longer than fifteen seconds to tick off such information, you might need to keep some slides on longer. But you should then consider breaking these long slides into several shorter ones, or using a "pop on" technique where slide A shows one fact; slide B shows the same fact plus one other; slide C shows everything that was on A and B, plus a third fact; etc. In this manner, you can eventually show on a single slide (the last in this grouping) all the material you require to explain your point—yet you have kept up the action while building to a climax.

WHAT OTHER VISUAL DEVICES CAN IMPROVE A PRESENTATION? The list is as big as your imagination and depends, naturally, upon the context and purpose of your talk. If you're introducing this season's line of men's shirts to a group of salesmen, you might have every item in the line on display behind you and stand beside each one as you describe it. If you're a physician talking about anatomy, perhaps you'll want a human skeleton with removable parts. If you're talking about how modern packaging gluts ecology, you could stand in front of twenty tables, each displaying different types of packages, and weave your talk around this visual material. If you're addressing a group of barbers, maybe you'll want to use live models. But apart from such special devices, there are several of a more general nature that have proven uncommonly successful in practice.

One spectacular use of visual props requires a room with cork boards all around it. Failing this, you can have special boards cut for you which can take tacks or two-sided tape and place these boards around two, three, or four sides of the room to create "a wall within a wall." The technique is to have all your visuals arranged, tacked up sequentially, and then covered over with large sheets of paper, actual sheeting, or cloth. As you give your talk, remove the coverings from the various sections of your displayed material (or, if you wish to stand in one place and speak from a podium up front, have an attractive assistant remove the coverings as you address the audience). When you have finished your presentation, your audience will literally be surrounded by a visual summary of all you have told them.

This same technique, in reverse, offers you an excellent device for building your visuals to a dramatic close. Instead of starting with all the visuals already in place, begin with blank walls or boards. Have an assistant tack up, or tape up, each visual as you talk about it. The tacking up of every point (either in key words or pictures) should be done *after* the point is made, not before, in order not to kill the suspense of your narration. When the talk is ready for summary or conclusions, you can move around the walls, using the now-posted visuals as aids in ticking off the points you have covered verbally. By the time you return to the lectern, you are ready for your closing lines.

There are a number of variations on these basic techniques for revealing or building up with visual props. For example, another way to reveal is to use a series of wooden venetian blinds and, as each point is made, turn down another slat of the blind on which key words are lettered. A more condensed version of the "build up" device is to purchase what is commonly known as a flannel board—a flocked display board to which cards of all shapes and sizes (some with pictures mounted on them, some with lettering) will easily and firmly adhere, after being fixed on the back with a magnetic gum that you can buy along with the flannel board. One or two such boards are usually sufficient to hold all the visual materials a speaker will want to "pop on" during an average-length presentation. Of course, all the suggestions made previously concerning the appearance and design of flip card visuals apply equally to the pictures and lettering that you use in this type of "build up."

Finally, a couple of short thoughts on using your aids to greatest advantage. Keep in mind that you're on the program to speak to the assembled audience—not to have a conversation with your visuals. It is surprising with what frequency public speakers unwittingly turn their backs on their audiences and address their visual material, face to face. It doesn't make the people out front curious about what's going on up there; it just turns them off.

Remember: since the audience has come to hear *you*, it just doesn't make sense to let your visual aids upstage you. After all, even if you do "make love to them," your visuals are still only supporting players. *You* are the star of the program!

THE 10 BEST
SPEECH BITS I'VE
EVER HEARD

guaranteed to get applause
from any audience

Ever so rarely, one hears a story or a line that is virtually timeless and almost certain to evoke the desired audience reaction—provided, of course, that the speaker delivers the material in such a way that his listeners fully understand both the punch line and what went before it. (Obviously, we can't expect an audience to respond to something it hasn't heard well enough to assimilate.) I've heard hundreds and hundreds of talks. And of the thousands of stories, allegories and punch lines in them that were delivered from the platform, there are only ten such bits I'd be willing to include in this category of immortals.)

I've personally used each of these ten gems a number of times in speeches I've ghosted. And, sitting in on the deliveries, I've never known any of them to fail. Nor did they receive mere trickles of response; they got everything from 100 per cent applause, or laughter, to standing ovations. Each of these ten items offers numerous possibilities for adaptation to special situations. And each of them is a winner that can also be used in social situations —as well as in public speeches—to make or climax a point, or to help a flagging conversation come alive. Here are my candidates for the ten best bits ever delivered from a platform.

¶

1. RUSSIAN FABLE

I think I can best make my point by telling you an old
Russian fable. A small bird lay freezing to death on a
country road in Russia. A peasant came along, saw the
dying bird, and thought to himself: "If only I had
something—anything—in which to wrap this bird, I
might save its life, for surely it is freezing to death."
But, unfortunately, he had nothing on him that he
could spare.

Nearby he caught sight of some cow droppings,
and he thought, in desperation, "Perhaps if I wrap the
bird in that, it will warm it enough to save its life." He
picked up the bird, wrapped it in the cow dung, laid it
gently on the ground, and went on his way. Sure

enough, the dung began to warm the bird, and it started to come to life again. The bird felt so overjoyed at feeling warm again that it attempted to sing. But all it could emit in its weakened condition were some low, pitiful notes.

Just then, another peasant came along. He heard the bird's attempt at song and thought, "Poor bird, it's strangulating in that cow dung." So he picked it up, removed the dung, laid the bird back on the ground, and—confident that he had saved its life—went on his way. Shortly thereafter, the bird died of the cold.

There are three morals to this fable. The first one is: It isn't necessarily your enemies who put you in it. The second one is: It isn't necessarily your friends who get you out of it. And the third moral is: When you're in it up to here, for God's sake, don't sing!

> There are many ways in which this Russian fable can be used in a talk. It might be used to summarize what has gone before. Or, it can be used after giving advice to people whose business or industry is beset by the problems of consumerism. It can be used appropriately when talking to, or about, politicians. Or, it can be used at the tail end of a talk after saying something like this: "I have been asked to give you my thoughts on [subject], which I have tried to do. And now, I'd like to throw in a piece of gratuitous advice, in the form of a Russian fable." As you go

through the draft of your own speech, perhaps you will find an even better way to work in this story.

¶

2. NO TWO WAYS ABOUT IT

A brave young man had just finished his period of training as a member of the Royal Canadian Mounted Police and, before he went off into the wilderness on his first assignment, his fellow Mounties gave him a farewell party. As a going-away gift, they gave him a complete martini-making set—a bottle of Canadian gin, some vermouth, a martini mixer, a stirrer, even a bottle of olives. The new Mountie thanked his friends most graciously, but he commented that he really didn't see a martini setup as a very appropriate gift for someone going off alone, into virtually unsettled territory, to search out a wanted criminal.

"Ah!" said one of his friends, a more experienced Mountie. "You'll find it to be a very important part of your equipment indeed. You may be out there in the vast wilderness, totally alone, for weeks or maybe even months. Sooner or later, you will yearn for the sound of another human voice. Then you will remember your martini set. You'll take it out, start to make yourself a martini, and in ten seconds flat there'll be someone at your shoulder saying, '*That's* not the way to make a martini!'"

This is one of the most serviceable stories around, because it can so easily be adapted to a host of activities other than martini-making. For example, a speaker might have occasion to say: "You may not like the way we planned this program. At meetings such as this, there is always someone who knows a better way. And that reminds me of the story about the young Canadian Mountie who . . ."

In addition to being awfully good in public speech, it's also an infallible way to put down someone who says to you, "*That's* not the way to build a fire!" or "*That's* not the way to barbecue chicken!" or in any of those other situations where people make it clear that they believe *their* way is better than *your* way.

¶

3. EAGER BEAVER

When Woodrow Wilson was Governor of New Jersey, a very ambitious young civil servant called him at his home at three thirty one morning and said urgently, "Mr. Governor, I'm sorry to wake you up, but your

State Auditor has just died and I would like to know if I can take his place."

Mr. Wilson thought that over for a moment and then replied dryly: "Well, I guess it's all right with me, if it's all right with the undertaker."

> Although this story is credited to Woodrow Wilson (there is no way of proving or disproving that he actually said it) it can be adapted to almost any political candidate: "People are so anxious to work on John Lindsay's team that, just the other day, an eager young politician awakened John at 3:30 A.M. and said, "Mr. Lindsay, sir, I heard that a member of your staff has just died, and I wonder if. . . ." The story can also be used to make a point about the many people who might be vying for a position on the Board of Directors of a big business firm, or on the board of a museum, school, or other civic organization; or, it can be nicely adapted to refer to the people on a college or university staff who are eager for promotion. In fact, there is almost no competitive situation where the eagerness of the competitors cannot be teased with the use of this anecdote.

¶

4. UPPER CRUST

The invitation to address you here today was accompanied by mixed emotions. On the one hand, I was pleased and flattered that you thought to ask me. On the other hand, I was somewhat intimidated by the thought of speaking to an audience that represents the upper crust in your field. I decided to accept the invitation, however, because—upon second thought—I realized that the upper crust is usually just a bunch of crumbs held together by dough!

In my experience, I have always found that this punch line elicits an appreciative response when the comment is made as part of the speaker's opening remarks. However, it works equally well in other contexts. For instance, a student, urging his peers to take action on some school issue, might tell them: "Don't be intimidated because we may have to take our request to the upper crust of the university hierarchy. After all, the upper crust . . ." A fund raiser, briefing his staff on how to make phone calls to potential donors, can say: "And don't get nervous just because you'll be calling the upper crust of this community. Just keep in mind that . . ."

Still another way to use the line is to "brush it off on someone else." If you don't know your audience makeup very well and are dubious about calling them "a bunch of crumbs held together by dough," you might say that you were somewhat nervous about appearing before the upper crust "until the program chairman reminded me that the upper crust is just . . ." etc.

¶

5. WHAT CAN YOU DO FOR ME LATELY?

A number of federal agencies are coming under scrutiny today, what with the many consumer advocates in Washington who want more action from some of these government bodies. One of those that has recently been under attack has been the Federal Communications Commission. Of course, not all of the FCC's problems come from the consumerists. When Newton Minow was head of it, he complained that he had a problem with his *mother*. She called him up and said: "Newton, since you've been in that job the television programs have really gotten much better. But can't you do anything about the TV dinners?"

Although this very effective anecdote takes off on a government agency, it is easy to bridge from the punch line to other operational groups. After giving Mrs. Minow's comment, the speaker can then say something like this: "We have the same problem in *our* business. After we put into effect all the quality controls, updated distribution, improved warranties, and easy-replacement policies that customers have been yelling about, they call us up and say, "But how come you didn't lower the price?"

The anecdote actually works in connection with any situation where you want to make the point that you simply can't do enough for certain people. And whether or not your audience is familiar with the problems of the FCC or has ever heard of Newton Minow makes no difference—audiences seem to get the point just the same.

¶

6. WOMAN'S AD LIB

A woman motorist was doing seventy miles an hour on a highway with a fifty-five mile speed limit. She happened to glance in her rearview mirror and spotted two state troopers on motorcycles as they pulled out from behind a billboard she had just passed. They seemed to be catching up with her, so she put her foot down on the gas and zoomed up to eighty miles an hour, with the cops in hot pursuit.

Down the road she spotted a service station. Gunning the motor, she roared into the station, drew to a screaming halt, jumped out of her car, and dashed into the ladies' room.

After a little while, she came out and saw the troopers flanking her car. She walked brightly over to where they were waiting and, with a big grin on her face, said: "You didn't think I'd make it, did you?"

This story is recommended for use if you or some other speaker is late in arriving, or if the program has gotten off to a late start. Then you might preface the story with a comment on how "our lateness in getting started puts me in mind of the woman motorist . . ."

However, the story has a fine track record when used in other ways as well. For example, it can be used at the end of your talk, after which you can say something to this effect: "We promised you this session would be over by noon, and I'm sure some, listening to me prattle on, didn't think we'd make it. Well, I have come to the end and we have made it— just in time for lunch."

In reviewing your own proposed talk, a bit of imagination will suggest other ways in which this story might serve you. A man talking about his industry's self-regulation—which was, perhaps, late in getting organized—could tie in with the punch line. A company president addressing his stockholders could use the tag line as an amusing way of getting across the point that the company had a profit and dividend objective, and that maybe some "didn't think we'd make it." In fact, any situation where there is doubt about whether an individual or a group or an organization "might make it" provides a perfect opportunity to use this certain laugh-getter.

¶

7. BIG BARGAIN

At the time of the last walk on the moon, a reporter asked one of the astronauts if he had been nervous when he was strapped into his seat before going into space.

"Well," he said, "of course I was. Who wouldn't be? There I was, sitting on top of 9,999 parts and bits—each of which had been made by the lowest bidder!"

> This quickie rejoinder gets a big hand, whether the audience is made up of businessmen, housewives, or anyone else. And it's easy to juggle into a place in your talk, whether your topic is the economy, the high cost of living, free enterprise, nervousness, reality testing, psychoanalysis, bargains, science, or capitalism *vs.* communism.

¶

8. PRESIDENTIAL SUITE

I simply have to tell you about the terrible experience I had when I got in town last night. I arrived at the hotel, went to the registration desk, and found that no room had been reserved for me even though I had written ahead for one.

I was a bit irritated and explained to the registration clerk that I was scheduled to speak here today, and it was essential that I have a place to sleep. There was a long line behind me, and the clerk was very harassed and he said: "Look, we'd certainly give you a room if we had one. There simply isn't a vacant room anywhere in the hotel."

I told him that I simply couldn't believe that. "Do you mean to say," I asked "that if Richard Nixon showed up, you'd turn him away? Wouldn't you manage to find him a room?"

"Well," admitted the clerk, "I guess if Mr. Nixon showed up we'd find a room for him somehow."

"Great!" I said, "Give me *his* room. He's not coming!"

This is an excellent story to use if you are speaking in a big and busy city that is not your home town, or if you're attending a convention at a resort which is very crowded. Everyone who goes to large meetings out of town has, at some time, had the experience of finding the hotel overbooked. It's also a pretty good story if you're abroad and speaking to a foreign audience that doesn't mind a bit of good-natured ribbing concerning its over-worked hotel facilities.

While this anecdote is very good in the opening position, it can also be used elsewhere in the talk. For example, if you're speaking to an audience in a city other than your own and want to say some nice things about the town, you might comment on the lovely airport, the friendly taxi drivers, the scenery, the downtown skyline, or a host of other appropriate things. Then, you might follow by saying: "However, I did have a bit of a scare when I arrived at the hotel last night. The clerk told me . . ."

Here's yet another way to use it. If you come from a big city such as New York, where out-of-towners find the natives less than friendly, you might run it in along these lines: "Yes, your city is delightful to look at, great to be in, and I must say I have found everyone to be a lot more friendly than you might find them when you come to visit me in [speaker's home town]. Why, just last week one of my friends was in from out of town, and when he arrived at his hotel . . ."

¶

9. POSITIVE THINKING

A scientist, unjustly accused and convicted of some major crime, found himself incarcerated with a long-term sentence in a jail in the midst of the desert. His cell mate turned out to be another scientist.

Determined to escape, the first man tried to convince his co-professional to make the attempt with him; but the man refused. After much planning, and with the undetected help of other inmates, our scientist made his escape.

But the heat of the desert, the lack of food and water, and his inability to locate another human being anywhere drove him almost mad, and he was forced to turn around and return to the jail. He reported his terrible experience to the other scientist, who surprised him by saying: "Yes, I know; I tried it and failed, too, for the same reasons."

The first scientist responded bitterly. "For heaven's sake, man, when you knew I was going to make a break for it, why didn't you tell me what it was like out there?"

To which his cell mate replied, with a shrug of the shoulders, "Who publishes negative results?"

> One does not need to be a scientist, or be addressing scientists, to use this story. I have heard it bring roars of laughter from housewives, from students, and from businessmen. In fact, I wrote it into a business executive's speech in the following manner. He was giving an annual report to the stockholders of the company he headed. First, he told all the good things that had happened to their company that

year. Then, he said: "Now, maybe you think everything in the last twelve months has been almost too good to be true. And perhaps you are remembering that great story about the scientist unjustly accused . . ." When the business executive said, "Who publishes negative results?" he all but brought down the house. And with the audience still laughing and chuckling, he went on to say: "I'm going to give you *all* the results of our last year's operation —including a few negative ones." After that, he presented the less happy side of the annual ledger. I truly think his stockholders took the bad news in good grace because of the delightful lead-in.

Similarly, the tale can be told by any appointed or elected official reporting to his community on a mixed bag of results from a specific program or campaign. It can be employed successfully by almost anyone—doctors, teachers, publishers, manufacturers, store executives, and, of course, researchers—reporting on some study or program that was recently concluded, with or without "negative results."

¶

10. THE LAST WORD

A man pulled off the highway and went into a roadside diner to have lunch. He ordered a hamburger, a cup of coffee, and a piece of pie. As his lunch was set before him, three rough-looking guys in leather jackets, motorcycle helmets, and boots entered the diner and sat down beside him at the counter. One grabbed his hamburger and ate it. Another grabbed his coffee and drank it, and the third tasted his pie, then mashed the rest of it on the plate.

The man said nothing, got up, paid the cashier for the food, and walked out. The three guys turned to the cashier, and one said: "Not much of a man, is he?"

"He's not much of a driver, either," said the cashier. "He just ran his truck over three motorcycles."

> These are just some of the points you can lead into from the truck driver story:
>
> > Silence speaks louder than words, particularly when accompanied by action.
> >
> > Speak softly—even better, not at all —and carry a big stick.
> >
> > It isn't always the loudmouth who has the last word.

Getting even; having the last word; tit-for-tat; a soft answer doesn't always turn away wrath—or hide it.

If you can't find a point in your talk where this tale fits in, save it. Tell it later, at lunch or over drinks or out on the golf course. I guarantee the laughter.

EXTRA MILEAGE FROM YOUR SPEECH

with a provocative title
and good publicity

If your invitation to do some public speaking comes ready-made with a title, and if it also happens to be a *good* one, count yourself lucky. Most often, you'll be told the subject of your talk (or asked to pick one yourself) and it will be up to you to come up with the title, along with the script.

Devising a title isn't difficult—almost any climactic sentence right out of the speech text could probably serve as a "handle." But an exciting and provocative title—and by that I mean one that arouses interest, anger, laughter, agreement, disagreement, or just plain curiosity—is going to help bring in a larger audience and get you press coverage and other publicity when the talk is over.

SHOULD YOU CREATE YOUR TITLE BEFORE OR AFTER YOU WRITE THE SPEECH? There's no rule, and it doesn't matter. Obviously, if a terrific title occurs to you right at the outset, you will have it in mind while thinking through your talk; and, as you write the script, you'll be able to "prove out" the title, or "make it fulfill its promise." But most speakers change titles several times before they settle on one—and, often, the best titles come right out of the script after it's been committed to paper.

HOW DO YOU THINK UP AN EXCITING TITLE? Once in a while, it will just "come to you"—which isn't as miraculous as it sounds. All those weeks of planning, researching, and thinking through your speech will have left your unconscious with a residue of ideas that will be stimulated into consciousness as you seek a title line to summarize your basic thesis or woo an audience. Sometimes, one of your favorite lines or phrases in the script will seem to stand out every time you read it, and you may feel it has enough built-in interest to make a good headline. But, often, you will need some special stimulus to get yourself thinking in the right direction. I usually start by "checking my p's and q's." Let me explain. I keep an index card in my desk drawer that has these words on it:

FOR TITLES
CHECK THESE P'S & Q'S

provoke
question
predict
quote

NEW SPEAKERS HANDBOOK · 378

praise

quip

paraphrase

pique quriosity

With these eight "clues" in front of me, I then go through my speech text several times, looking for ways in which I can provoke interest or disagreement, ask a question, make a prediction, pick up a quotation, come out in praise of an idea or person, use humor, take off on someone's phraseology (maybe my own), or arouse curiosity concerning the subject of my talk.

These examples will show you the sort of titles that could result from "checking your P's & Q's":

PROVOKE: The Governor Must Be Impeached!

Let's Do Away with Examinations!

It's Time We Repealed This Town's Zoning Laws!

QUESTION: Why Socialized Medicine?

Is "Made in U.S.A." Passé?

Should Our Drug Laws Be Changed?

PREDICT: Open Admissions: The Trend of the Future

We're Going to Destroy Every River in the Land!

Japan: The Number-One Industrial Power of the Eighties?

QUOTE: "Ask What You Can Do for Your Country"

"Creativity Is the Sudden Cessation of Stupidity"

Consumerism: "An Idea Whose Time Has Come"

NOTE: Often, an excellent title will come from quoting a line of your own, lifted right out of the text of your speech.

PRAISE: Long Live Andy Warhol!

How Group Therapy Saved My Marriage

Weight Watchers to the Rescue!

QUIP: It Only Hurts When I Laugh—The Story of My Transplant

Equal Rights for the Better Half

My Son the Nurse

PARAPHRASE: How to Fail in the Stock Market Without Hardly Trying

Caveat Vendor—Let the Seller Beware!

A Funny Thing Happened to Me on the Way to City Hall (A talk by a defeated candidate)

PIQUE
QURIOSITY: A Message to the Colonies: The Beatles Are Dead!

A New Pay-out Plan for Stockholders

Why I Am Resigning as University President

SHOULD A SPEECH TITLE BE LONG OR SHORT? If the program chairman advises you that the title of your talk should be "one line," or "eight words or less," tell him to forget it! As with the modern book or play, the important thing is whether or not the words *fulfill their function as a title*—not whether they conform to someone's concept of proper length. One of the most successful and best publicized talks ever given by Stephen O. Frankfurt when he was the youthful president of the Young & Rubicam advertising agency was titled: "STEPHEN O. FRANKFURT PRESENTS ED SULLIVAN, ARTHUR GODFREY AND ANDY WARHOL IN 'THE DECLINE & FALL OF THE HOLY GRAIL.'" Although all the members of the Hollywood Radio & Television Society, before whom the talk was to be given, knew that Sullivan, Godfrey and Warhol were not going to appear, Mr. Frankfurt's advance notices—which gave only the title and divulged nothing of the talk's content—brought out a record-breaking crowd. The title had nineteen words in it, but it did a fine job of piquing curiosity and alerting the audience to the likelihood that this would be an amusing talk.

Very short titles are also so unusual as to stand out in a printed program. I remember one clever twist involving a short title. The Membership Chairman of the New York Sales Executive Club was listed as one of the speakers at one of their luncheons. Next to his name on the program appeared only the words "An Appeal." Knowing that the Membership Chairman's job was to increase membership, the audience was understandably restless and barely tolerant when it came time for him to make his remarks. Were it not that the door prizes were still to be awarded, it is likely that many in the audience might have walked out at that point. After a somber introduction that included the chairman's plea for careful attention to this serious part of the program, the Membership Chairman arose, conspicuously organized a thick sheaf of papers he held in his hand, waited for total silence in the room, and —dramatically gripping the microphone—cried, "Join!" and sat down. The applause was thunderous.

WHEN YOU'VE DECIDED ON YOUR TITLE, play devil's advocate with yourself. Try to determine if it's the right sort of title for the members of your potential audience. Is your title on target for their age, education, orientation?

Why are they there? For a laugh? To learn? To debate? What are their problems? What is likely to make them angry? What will make them laugh? Most of all, ask yourself if the audience, as best you can create its profile, is likely to be responsive to a talk that is pre-heralded with the "headline" you've selected.

THE TITLE GIVES YOU A BIG ADVANTAGE OVER THE REST OF YOUR SCRIPT. You will not need to *say* the words in it unless you choose to do so. Everything else in your speech should be written for the *ear* to pick up, but your title can be created for the *eye*. The person who introduces you to the audience will probably state your speech title, and *that is the only time it will be voiced*. Therefore, the title words you pick need not necessarily "be you"; they need not be words you would be likely to use in talking. On the other hand, your title should *read* well because it will appear in programs, advance notices, press reports, etc. So, approach your title problem as you would if you had written a book, magazine article, play, or movie. And whatever title you go with, remember that you owe it to your audience to either explain it or make it "pay out" during the talk. Otherwise, some members of the audience might feel they didn't get what they had been led to expect.

YOU CAN INCREASE THE AUDIENCE FOR YOUR MESSAGE by publicizing it—before and after the talk is delivered. After all, you've worked long and hard to put together a meaningful and perhaps important speech. Why let it die after delivery? The hardest work is behind you. You deserve extra mileage for your efforts, and publicity is the medium through which you can get it.

THE NOTICES ABOUT YOUR TALK SHOULD GO OUT FAR ENOUGH IN ADVANCE to assure a large audience—large in terms of the room in which you will speak. It's depressing to speaker *and* audience if only a few seats in the room are occupied. You're better off with a small room and an overflow crowd than with a large auditorium only one-third filled.

When you accept your invitation to speak, ask the person who invited you how large an audience can be expected and what means will be used to publicize your talk in advance. Customarily, the sponsoring group will send out a mailing that announces your forthcoming appearance. If the audience is also to be drawn from the general public, a notice or advance press release should be sent to local newspapers. If the audience is to be a specialized one, then press releases will usually go to relevant trade or professional publications.

If you're not acquainted with the publicity capabilities of the group sponsoring your talk, it is perfectly permissible for you to ask to see the press releases and advance notices before they go out and to request that your name be added to the mailing list. This will give you a first-hand check on when the advance publicity has gone out. If you get close to the speaking date and have not seen any notices in your mail, don't hesitate to phone the program chairman and make a polite inquiry. Even well-intentioned groups sometimes slip up between the plan and the follow-through. If you're going to take seriously the job of preparing an outstanding speech, you have every right to expect the sponsoring group to deliver an audience.

In addition to advance press releases, which should contain some clue to the content of your proposed talk as well as a bit of biographical information, interest can be stimulated and audiences can be built by phone calls to local club chairmen, by posting bulletin board notices in clubs and business offices where potential audience members might see them, and by notifications sent to local radio stations for use on their "community billboard of the air" or in their public service announcements.

AFTER THE SPEECH IS OVER AND THE APPLAUSE HAS DIED DOWN, you can enjoy extra payout and give longer life to your words by utilizing some of the techniques employed by professional public relations people. Here are the most frequently used devices:

Press Releases, containing the most important ideas in your talk, are a "must." They should open with a dramatic statement or a provocative passage taken from your text, much as a newspaper story will give the most significant aspect of the news in the opening lines. All the newsworthy parts of your talk should be quoted in the release, and a bit of biographical information should establish your credentials as a speaker on this particular subject. These releases should be made available to members of the press immediately after your talk is completed (or just before it, if reporters have imminent deadlines). Phone calls alerting the press to these releases should be made by someone on your staff, or by the sponsoring group—not by you.

Press Conferences give you an opportunity, in person, to amplify or expand on some of your speech ideas. However, in order to get members of the press corps to attend such a conference, you must be a VIP, or the subject matter of your talk must be of vital concern to the readers of their publications or the listeners to their stations. In small towns, where there may be only one newspaper, it is easier to arrange a press interview at the newspaper's offices. If your remarks could be of significance in cities other than the one where you are speaking, be sure that members of the national press corps (U.P.I., A.P., and the networks) have also been invited to your conference.

Copies of Your Complete Text can carry your message into many homes, offices, and classrooms if such copies are made available to interested persons. They can also serve to get added attention from people who heard you talk, and want to give further thought to your comments or pass them along to others in their organizations. There are several good ways to distribute such copies:

¶ Have copies of your talk available to everyone who heard you speak. They should either be waiting at the back of the room when your address is over, or mailed to audience members who leave their names and addresses.

¶ Mail copies of the complete text to thought leaders, along with a short note from you inviting their comments.

¶ Send copies to radio and television commentators and to the editors of appropriate print media.

Reprints of Your Talk in Small Booklet Form can be used for mailing purposes instead of the less expensive (but less impressive) "duplicated" variety. While the ordinary mimeographed or office-reproduced copies convey a feeling of immediacy (and are, therefore, excellent for the press), the printed booklet lends an air of importance to the text. In such printed form, your talk, along with a covering letter, could make an excellent mailing piece to be sent to prospects, clients, community leaders, or any other group you wish to reach with your ideas.

Magazine Reprints of Your Speech bring still another audience to your message. If there is any publication that serves an audience which could be interested in your comments, send a copy of your talk to the editor and offer to edit the copy for publication, should the magazine agree to carry it. Such editing is usually a simple job (unless your talk is heavily dependent upon visual material— in which case an interested publication will usually offer you assistance in turning your visuals into printworthy illustrations) and well worth the small amount of additional work, since your ideas might then be carried to many times the number of people who heard you in person.

Repeating Your Talk Before Other Groups is still another way to increase the return on your investment in time and effort. Once you know that you have a good speech and that you've been successful in communicating your ideas to an audience, it becomes easier and easier to deliver that same talk, sometimes with minor variations to suit your new listeners. I know famous personalities who have given the same speech, or versions of it, to as many as fifteen or twenty different audiences. (Of course politicians, during an election campaign, frequently give but a single speech, over and over again, to every audience they address.) There is nothing wrong with this. If your message is still valid, if the audience hasn't heard the talk before, and if you can fulfill a program need, why not put all that hard work to use again? Just be sure you don't go stale and "walk through" your tenth delivery—your audience will detect your own boredom at once.

A Digest of Your Speech, picking up the salient ideas and the most readable phraseology, can bring the essence of your address to still other audiences. Writing such a digest is not difficult; it's a pick-and-choose process, with perhaps some new sentences to bridge the ideas and tie them together. Such a digest can be used as a mailing to clients, prospects, friends, and association members, or as an interoffice or inter-staff memo.

Whichever of the above reprint techniques you use, be certain to give it the widest possible distribution. Think in terms of mailing lists to VIPs; campus and student publications; the Chamber of Commerce; the staffs of schools, hospitals, businesses, etc.; political clubs, women's groups, fraternal organizations, and trade and professional groups.

Your efforts in striving to create a title worthy of your speech, and your publicity activities, will bring big dividends. All your thought and work in creating a great speech will pay off many times over. If you have used the material in this book to spice up your text and make it more memorable, and if you have sharpened and rehearsed your delivery as described in the chapter "Your Speech Will Almost Write Itself," you are bound to experience the thrill that every public speaker knows when the audience breaks into spontaneous and sustained applause. Long after you have left the platform, you will hear the sound of this acclaim ringing in your ears.

And with the right sort of publicity, you will continue to get calls and mail from people who have an opportunity to read about, or hear about, your speech—or, better yet, to read the speech itself. Don't be surprised if, months after you make your platform appearance, someone writes you for a copy of "that fine talk I've heard so much about, and would like to read for myself." Chalk it up as one of the justly deserved rewards that come to every public speaker who has learned how easy it is to be *the life of the podium.*

BIOGRAPHICAL INDEX

HOW TO USE THIS INDEX
to document your speech

This index contains thumbnail identifications of each person quoted directly in *New Speakers Handbook.*

You may, in going through the book, find quotations you would like to include in your talk—but perhaps the persons quoted are unfamiliar, or only vaguely familiar, to you. By checking their thumbnail biographies here, you can find out when they lived (or, if still alive, their age) and their principal claims to fame. Should you need more information, you can, of course, refer to such library sources as *Who's Who* and various biographical dictionaries and encyclopedias. But the chances are that the data you find here will be sufficient for the average reference.

Sometimes you may feel that a person quoted might be unfamiliar to your audience. That shouldn't stop you from using the quote. You can identify the person with a brief reference, such as: "Otto Loewi, the German pharmacologist who won the Nobel Prize, once said . . . " or, "Edwin Land, who—as you probably know—invented the Polaroid camera, was once known to remark . . . " Even with so brief an identification, your audience will accept the fact that the person quoted has acceptable credentials for fame.

There may be other instances where you like a quotation but prefer not to use the name of the person who first made the quoted statement. It is perfectly proper for you to use the passage without specific credit, provided you indicate that you are quoting someone—that the passage is not original with you. The way to handle a situation like that is to say, "A well-known banker once said . . . " or, "More than two hundred years ago, a philosopher expressed it this way . . . "

Being clued in on a few facts about the person you're quoting will give you greater self-confidence in using this material. It will also establish for your audience that you are well read and well prepared for your platform appearance. All this is bound to reflect favorably upon your reputation as a speaker, and will give your listeners additional reason to respect your points of view.

ADDISON, JOSEPH (1672–1719). English essayist, poet, statesman. Contributor, *The Tatler* and *The Spectator*.

ALEXANDER THE GREAT (Alexander III) (356–323 B.C.). Ruler of Greece. Founded Alexandria, conquered Thrace and Illyria, destroyed Thebes.

ARISTOTLE (384–322 B.C.). Greek philosopher; tutored Alexander the Great. Author, *Sophisms, Metaphysics,* etc.

AURELIUS, MARCUS (A.D. 121–180). Roman emperor from 161 to 180 and Stoic philosopher.

BARNETT, HOMER GARNER (1906–). Educator and anthropologist. Author, *Innovation: The Basis of Cultural Change.*

BILLINGS, JOHN SHAW (1838–1913). Physician and librarian. Chief Librarian, New York Public Library, 1896–1913.

BRANDEIS, LOUIS DEMBITZ (1856–1941). American jurist and Associate Justice, U.S. Supreme Court. Author, *The Curse of Bigness.*

BRYAN, WILLIAM JENNINGS (1860–1925). American lawyer and political leader; known as "the Commoner." Thrice defeated in bid for Presidency.

CAPP, AL (1909–). Cartoonist, columnist, author of comic strip "Li'l Abner."

CARLYLE, THOMAS (1795–1881). Scottish essayist, historian, lecturer. Attacked shams and corruption. Author, *Past and Present, Oliver Cromwell.*

CARNEGIE, DALE (1888–1955). Writer and instructor in public speaking. Author, *How to Win Friends and Influence People.*

CARROLL, LEWIS (pseudonym of Charles L. Dodgson) (1832–1898). English mathematician and writer. Author, *Alice's Adventures in Wonderland, Through the Looking Glass.*

CHAPMAN, JOHN JAY (1862–1933). American essayist, playwright, lawyer. Author, *Emerson and Other Essays.*

CHURCHILL, SIR WINSTON LEONARD SPENCER (1874–1965). British statesman and author. Prime Minister, 1940–45 and 1951–55. Led country to victory in World War II.

CICERO, MARCUS TULLIUS (106–43 B.C.). Roman orator, statesman, philosopher. Famous for orations against Catiline.

CLARK, MARK WAYNE (1896–). Five-star Army general famous for his World War II victories in Italy. Allied chief, Italy, 1944–45. Chief, U.S. Forces in Austria, 1945–47.

COLTON, CHARLES CALBE (1780?–1832). English clergyman, sportsman, wine merchant. Author, *Lacon*.

CONFUCIUS (551–479 B.C.). Latinized form of Kung Fu-tse ("Philosopher Kung"). Chinese utilitarian philosopher born Kufow, State of Lu (now Shantung Province) who called himself "a transmitter, not an originator." Devoted to study of ancient writings. Prime Minister of Lu. Wandered 12 years from state to state teaching morals, family system, social reforms, statecraft. His maxims became guide for people's daily lives.

COOLIDGE, JOHN CALVIN (1872–1933). Thirtieth President of the U.S. Succeeded to Presidency on death of Harding, 1923; elected President, 1924.

CURIE, PIERRE (1859–1906). French chemist. Known especially for work with his wife on radioactivity, leading to their discovery of the elements polonium and radium. Won Nobel Prize in physics, 1903.

DEPEW, CHAUNCEY MITCHELL (1834–1928). Lawyer and U.S. Senator. President, N.Y. Central Railroad, 1885–99. Renowned after-dinner speaker.

DE VRIES, PETER (1910–). Writer, editor, novelist. Staff of *New Yorker* magazine. Author, *The Tunnel of Love* and many others.

DEWAR, THOMAS ROBERT (1864–1930). First Baron Dewar of Homestall. British distiller, sportsman, and raconteur. Author, *Ramble Around the Globe.*

DIOGENES (412?–323 B.C.). Greek Cynic philosopher who rejected social conventions, lived in a tub, and went through the streets with a lantern "looking for an honest man."

DISRAELI, BENJAMIN (1804–1881). First Earl of Beaconsfield. Prime Minister of Great Britain, author, and intimate friend of Queen Victoria.

DULLES, JOHN FOSTER (1888–1959). Lawyer; U.S. Secretary of State, 1953–59. American representative at Berlin Debt Conferences, 1933.

DUNNE, FINLEY PETER (1867–1936). American humorist and newspaperman. Editor, *Chicago Journal.* Creator of saloon-keeper-philospher "Mr. Dooley."

DU VALL, KENNETH KEITH (1900–). American banker. President and director, First National Bank of Appleton, Wis. and director, Merchandise National Bank of Chicago.

EDISON, THOMAS ALVA (1847–1931). American inventor who patented more than 1,000 inventions, including phonograph, automatic telegraph repeater, mimeograph, the Ediphone, the incandescent electric lamp, etc.

ELIOT, CHARLES WILLIAM (1834–1926). Mathematician; president, Harvard University, 1869–1909. Editor, *Harvard Classics.* Author, *The Happy Life.*

EMERSON, RALPH WALDO (1803–1882). Essayist, poet, Unitarian minister, and anti-slavery lecturer. Author, *The Conduct of*

Life.

FRANKFURT, STEPHEN OWEN (1931–). Communications executive and president, Young & Rubicam advertising agency, 1968–71.

GARDNER, JOHN W. (1912–). Secretary, Department of Health, Education and Welfare, 1965–68. Founder, Common Cause. Director, Woodrow Wilson Foundation.

GINZBERG, ELI (1911–). Economist, educator, government consultant, author. Served in Departments of Labor, Defense, Commerce, and State in 1950s and '60s.

GLENN, JOHN HERSCHEL Jr. (1921–). Astronaut; first American in orbit, 1962. Circled the earth three times in Mercury capsule "Friendship 7."

GOETHE, JOHANN WOLFGANG VON (1749–1832). German poet and writer. Author, *Faust, Egmont,* etc. Inaugurated German literary movement known as "Sturm und Drang."

GOLDWYN, SAMUEL (né Goldfish) (1882–). Motion picture producer and founder of Metro-Goldwyn-Mayer Corp. Pioneer in hiring famous writers to do film scripts.

GOSSAGE, HOWARD (1919–1970). West coast advertising executive. Co-founder, Wiener & Gossage Advertising Agency.

GRAVES, CHARLES (1899–). British chronicler, historian, and world traveler. Author, *Fourteen Islands in the Sun.*

HAMILTON, EDITH (1867–1963). American classical scholar and writer. Specialist in Greek, Roman, and Hebrew philosophy. Author, *The Greek Way.*

HAMMARSKJÖLD, DAG (1905–1961). Swedish diplomat and first Secretary General of the U.N. Killed in plane crash while on U.N. mission to Northern Rhodesia.

HAZARD, ELLISON LOCKWOOD (1911–). Business leader and president of Continental Can Co., which he in joined 1934.

HEROPHILUS (circa 300 B.C.). Greek anatomist and surgeon. Founder of first school of anatomy in Alexandria. First to conduct postmortems.

HOBSON, JOHN (1858–1940). English economist. Author, *Problems of Poverty, The Evolution of Modern Capitalism.*

HOLMES, OLIVER WENDELL (1809–1894). American man of letters and sometimes practicing physician. Professor of anatomy at Dartmouth. Author, *The Autocrat of the Breakfast Table, The Chambered Nautilus.*

HUGO, VICTOR MARIE (1802–1885). French playwright, novelist and poet, and leader of the Romantic movement in French literature. Author, *Les Misérables.*

JARRELL, RANDALL (1914–1965). American poet, essayist and teacher. Author, *Blood for a Stranger, Little Friend, Little Friend.*

JEFFERSON, THOMAS (1743–1826). Third President of the U.S., 1801–09. Drafted and signed the Declaration of Independence.

JOHNSON, LYNDON BAINES (1908–). Thirty-sixth President of the U.S. Succeeded to Presidency upon assassination of President Kennedy, 1963. Elected President in 1964.

JOHNSON, SAMUEL (1709–1784). English lexicographer, critic,

and conversationalist. Known as "Dr. Johnson" (held LLD degrees). Edited *The Rambler.*

KAPLAN, MAX (1911–). Director of Arts Center, Boston University. Author, *Leisure in America: A Social Inquiry,* and *Music in the City.*

KENNEDY, JOHN FITZGERALD (1917–1963). Thirty-fifth president of the U.S., assassinated in 1963 while serving his first term. Author of *Profiles in Courage,* which won Pulitzer Prize for biography.

KHRUSHCHEV, NIKITA SERGEEVICH (1894–1971). Russian political leader. Named First Secretary of the Communist Party, 1953; Premier of Soviet Union, 1958; ousted, 1964, after de-Stalinizing Russia. Lived in seclusion from then until his death.

LAMB, CHARLES (1775–1834). English essayist and critic. At times confined to mental institution. Author, *A Tale of Rosamund Gray, John Woodvil.*

LAND, EDWIN HERBERT (1909–). Inventor and corporate executive. Invented polarizing filter for cameras and the Polaroid camera.

LA ROCHEFOUCAULD, DUC FRANÇOIS DE (1613–1680). French writer. Author, *Reflexions ou Sentences et Maximes Morales.*

LEACOCK, STEPHEN BUTLER (1869–1944). Canadian economist, writer and humorist. Head of Economics Department, McGill University. Author, *Nonsense Novels, My Remarkable Uncle.*

LEAHY, (Sylvester Francis) FRANK (1909–). Utilities executive who started at the bottom with Detroit Edison Co. (1931) and rose to vice president for employee and union relations (1961). Director, Leahy Co.

LINDSAY, JOHN VLIET (1921–). Mayor, New York City 1965– . Republican Congressman, 86th–89th Congress. Sought presidential nomination, 1972.

LIVY (Titus Livius) (59 B.C.–A.D. 17). Roman historian and writer. Under patronage of Emperor Augustus, wrote history of Rome, from its foundations to 9 B.C. Younger brother of Emperor Tiberius.

LOEWI, OTTO (1873–1961). German-born pharmacologist. Shared with Sir Henry Hallett the 1936 Nobel Prize for physiology and medicine.

LONGFELLOW, HENRY WADSWORTH (1807–1882). American poet and professor of modern languages. Author, *The Village Blacksmith, The Song of Hiawatha, The Courtship of Miles Standish.*

MACLEISH, ARCHIBALD (1892–). American poet, essayist, librarian. Assistant Secretary of State, 1944–45. Author of *Conquistador*, for which he won Pulitzer Prize.

MACMILLAN, HAROLD (1894–). British Prime Minister, 1957–63.

MAHER, EDWARD (1902–). Editor, publisher, radio commentator, and public relations executive. Assistant publisher and editor, *Liberty Magazine.* Vice president for public relations for National Association of Manufacturers.

MAO TSE-TUNG (1893–). First Chairman of the People's Republic of China. Son of peasant farmer, helped found Chinese Communist Party and set up Chinese Soviet Republic in South East

China. Defied attacks of Chiang Kai-shek's forces; resisted the Japanese and proclaimed People's Republic in 1949. Chairman of party Politburo. Author: *New Democracy, On a Prolonged War,* "Little Red Book" of Chairman Mao's Sayings.

MASSON, THOMAS LANSING (1866–1934). Humorist, editor, author, associate editor, *Saturday Evening Post* and managing editor, *Life* magazine. Author, *A Bachelor's Baby.*

MEAD, MARGARET (1901–). American anthropologist. Made expeditions to New Guinea and Bali. Author, *Coming of Age in Samoa, Growing Up in New Guinea, Male and Female.*

MEDLICOTT, SIR FRANK (1903–). British solicitor who served with the Ministry of Health in 1943. Knighted, 1955.

MENCKEN, H. L. (Henry Louis) (1880–1956). American editor and satirist. Founded, with George Jean Nathan, and edited, *The American Mercury.* Author, *New Dictionary of Quotations.*

MINOW, NEWTON NORMAN (1926–). Lawyer and Chairman of the Federal Communications Commission, 1961–63.

MIZNER, WILSON (1876–1933). Dramatist, short story writer, Hollywood script writer, and occasional real estate entrepreneur.

MORLEY, JOHN (Viscount) (1838–1923). English statesman and man of letters. Editor, *Fortnightly Review* and *Pall Mall.* Secretary of State for India, 1905–10. Author, *Edmund Burke, Life of Gladstone.*

MULLER, LAWRENCE J. (1919–). Writer and advertising executive. Founder of Warren, Muller, Dolobowsky New York advertising agency.

MUSKIE, EDMUND SIXTUS (1914–). Governor of Maine, U.S. Senator, unsuccessful candidate for the U.S. vice presidency, 1968. Sought Democratic presidential nomination, 1972.

NADER, RALPH (1934–). Lawyer, author, and leader of the consumer movement of the 1960s and '70s. Author, *Unsafe at Any Speed.*

NEHRU, JAWAHARLAL (1889–1964). First Prime Minister of India, 1947–64. Successor to Gandhi as leader of India's National Congress Party. Served 5½ years in jail for his nationalist activities.

NEUMANN, HANS H., M.D. (1911–). Director of Preventive Medicine, City of New Haven, Connecticut. Popular lecturer and writer on problems of drug abuse, social diseases, health care systems. Author, *Foreign Travel Immunization Manual.*

OLIVER, ANDREW (1706–1774). American colonial political leader. Lieutenant Governor of Massachusetts and Secretary of the Province. Unpopular, and hanged in effigy.

OPPENHEIMER, J. ROBERT (1904–1967). American physicist instrumental in development of the atom bomb. Associated with the Institute for Advanced Study at Princeton. Contributed to development of quantum theory.

OSBORN, HENRY FAIRFIELD (1887–1935). American naturalist and conservationist. President, N.Y. Zoological Society; chairman of the board, Conservation Foundation. Author, *Our Plundered Planet.*

PRATT, THEODORE (1901–). Author and freelance journalist. Wrote novels, plays, short stories, motion picture scripts, and articles. Author, *Escape to Eden, The White God.*

PRIESTLEY, JOHN BOYNTON (1894–). English novelist, critic, and playwright. Author, *George Meredith, Let the People Sing.*

ROCKEFELLER, DAVID (1915–). Banker. Director and chairman of the board, Chase Manhattan Bank. Chairman of the board, Chase International Investment Corp.

ROCKEFELLER, JOHN DAVISON, III (1906–). Chairman, Board of Trustees, Rockefeller Foundation. Former chairman, Board of Trustees, Population Council.

ROCKWELL, WILLARD FREDERICK, JR. (1914–). Manufacturing executive, and president and chief executive officer, Rockwell Manufacturing Co.

ROGERS, WILL (William Penn Adair) (1879–1935). Actor, lecturer, humorist, vaudevillian. Starred in motion pictures, wrote syndicated newspaper articles. Killed in plane crash.

ROOSEVELT, (Anna) ELEANOR (1884–1962). Author, lecturer, and delegate to the U.N. Wife of President Franklin D. Roosevelt. Author, *On My Own, This I Remember,* and the column, "My Day."

ROOSEVELT, FRANKLIN DELANO (1882–1945). Thirty-second President of the U.S., and first President to be elected for a third term (1933–45). Known for his New Deal legislation. Author, *Whither Bound, Looking Forward.*

ROOSEVELT, THEODORE (1858–1919). Twenty-sixth President of the U.S. Succeeded to the Presidency on death of McKinley, 1901; elected President, 1904.

RUBICAM, RAYMOND (1892–). Retired advertising executive and co-founder of Young & Rubicam, Inc., advertising agency.

RUSKIN, JOHN (1819–1900). English art critic and sociological writer. Author, *The Art of England, Modern Painters, Ethics of the Dust.*

SAROYAN, WILLIAM (1908–). American fiction writer and playwright. Author, *The Daring Young Man on the Flying Trapeze, The Time of Your Life, My Heart's in the Highlands.*

SEAVER, THOMAS (1944–). Professional baseball player with the Mets. Vietnam antiwar speaker.

STEVENSON, ADLAI EWING (1900–1965). U.S. Ambassador to the U.N., Governor of Illinois, 1949–53. Unsuccessful candidate for the Presidency in 1952 and 1956.

SUSSKIND, DAVID HOWARD (1920–). Television, motion picture, Broadway theatrical producer. Co-owner, president, Talent Associates, Ltd. Moderator TV discussion programs "Open End," "The David Susskind Show." Produced TV's "Philco Playhouse," "Kraft Theater," "Armstrong Circle Theater," others. Producer of many movies including *Edge of the City, Raisin in The Sun, All the Way Home, Lovers and Other Strangers.* Recipient of numerous industry awards.

SWANN, DONALD (1923–). British actor, composer and performer in musicals. Appeared in *At the Drop of a Hat* and frequently in productions with Michael Flanders.

THACKERAY, WILLIAM MAKEPEACE (1811–1863). English novelist and journalist. Frequent contributor to *Punch.* Author, *Vanity Fair, Pendennis, Henry Esmond.*

THOMAS, NORMAN (1884–1968). American socialist politician and unsuccessful presidential candidate on Socialist ticket in five elections, 1928–44. Ordained a Presbyterian minister but resigned. Associate Editor, *The Nation.*

THORNTON, CHARLES BATES ("Tex") (1913–). Electronics manufacturer and chairman of the board, Litton Industries. Former executive, Hughes Aircraft and Hughes Tool Co.

THURBER, JAMES (1894–1961). American artist and writer, famous for his cartoons in the *New Yorker,* of which he was managing editor. Author, *Is Sex Necessary?, My Life and Hard Times, The Middle-Aged Man on the Flying Trapeze,*

TOLSTOI, COUNT LEV (Leo) NIKOLAEVICH (1828–1910). Russian novelist, social and moral philosopher, and religious mystic. Founder of Tolstoyism.

TRUEBLOOD, (David) ELTON (1900–). College professor, philosopher, writer. Associated with Harvard, Stanford, Swarthmore, Earlham College. Taught religion and philosophy. With U.S.I.A., 1954–5.

TURNER, RALPH HERBERT (1919–). Educator and sociologist. Editor, *American Journal of Sociology;* editor, *Sociology and Social Reserach.* Author, *The Social Context of Ambition.*

TWAIN, MARK (pseudonym of Samuel L. Clemens) (1835–1910). American humorist and writer. Author, *The Adventures of Tom Sawyer, The Prince and the Pauper, Adventures of Huckleberry Finn, A Connecticut Yankee in King Arthur's Court.*

VOLTAIRE (assumed name of François Marie Arouet) (1694–1778). French writer of satire who was imprisoned in the Bastille, where he wrote the tragedy *Oedipe.* Defender of victims of religious intolerance. Author, *Le Dictionnaire Philosophique.*

VON BRAUN, WERNHER (1912–). German-born engineer and rocket specialist. Responsible for development of V-2 long range rocket. Chief, Guided Missile Development Division, 1950–56. Specialist in liquid fuel rockets, rocket design, and power plants for guided missiles.

WEST, DAME REBECCA (pseudonym of Cicily Isabel Fairfield) (1892–). English novelist; author, *Henry James, The Birds Fall Down, Return of the Soldier,* and many others.

WILSON, (Thomas) WOODROW (1856–1924). Twenty-eighth President of the U.S., 1913–21. Previously, Governor of New Jersey. Awarded Nobel Peace Prize, 1919.

WIRTZ, WILLIAM WILLARD (1912–). Government official and former Secretary of Labor. With War Labor Board, 1943–45. Chairman of National Wage Stabilization Board, 1946.

WRIGHT, FRANK LLOYD (1869–1959). American architect. Innovator of striking designs in private dwellings and public and quasi-public buildings. Among his best-known works was the old Imperial Hotel in Tokyo. Founder of the Taliesin Fellowship, a cultural experiment in the arts.

SUBJECT INDEX

**HOW TO USE THIS INDEX
to prepare a better speech**

This is more than an ordinary index, more than a mere listing of where to find what in the book—although it is that, too. It is a valuable tool to help you write a sharper and livelier talk.

In looking for interesting material with which to enliven your speech, first check the Table of Contents for those chapters which might have pertinent material. After selecting your items from those chapters, check this Index for words which are the same as, or similar to, the chapter heading. There's good reason for doing that. If, for example, you're writing a business talk and have excerpted from the chapter on "Business" what you want to use, you should then check the word "business" in this Index. Under that word, you will find page numbers for other business-related items scattered throughout the book. For example, you will be referred to business selections in the chapters on "Openers," "Youth," and, of course, "Industry Chiefs."

If you can still use additional material, run your eye down *this entire Index* to find key words that suggest related items. In the case of a talk on business, you will find in the Index the word "selling". This will refer you to material in the chapters on "Advertising," "Facts, Figures and Reserach," "Proverbs," "One-Liners," and "Kennedy, Churchill and Stevenson"—all business-related items. Many of these may be pertinent to the subject of your talk. Depending upon what aspect of business you're addressing yourself to, you might also find relevant references under such Index words as "change," "cities," "prophesying," "women," "problem-solving," "leadership," and many others.

Regardless of the subject of your talk, you should use the same procedure. If you're preparing a speech on a topic such as "Women's Lib," for which there is no specific chapter in this book, the Index will give you references under words such as "women," "achievement," "success," "action," "children," "marriage," "knowledge," "egotism," "equality" and many, many more.

Were you readying a speech on the subject of travel, there might be helpful material for you in the references for the words "conventions," "hotels," "wealth," "skeptics," "Englishmen," "Frenchmen," "Russians," "children," etc. etc.

So don't short change yourself. Use this Index. Browsing it may suggest numerous categories of appropriate material that might not otherwise have occurred to you.

babies. *See* children
bankers 202
bargains 93, 104, 366
bastards 286
beards 229
beginnings 215, 224, 226, 231, 332
bias 331
Bible 62, 70
blindness 285
blood 257
boredom 324
borrowing 223
Boy Scouts 26, 72, 329. *See also* Girl
  Scouts
bravery 298. *See also* courage
builder 299
business 19, 78. *See also* "Doctors,
  Lawyers, Industry Chiefs," 185–
  205

candid 262
captivity 299
cars 60, 73
change 121, 135, 250, 262, 311, 327
character 281
charity 284
charts. *See* "Making Love to Your
  Visuals," 337–351
Chesterfield, Lord (P.D. Stanhope) 33
children 79, 80, 83, 85, 116, 117, 193,
  225, 249, 269
China 275–279, 300
Chinese 248, 275–279
choice 219
cities 123, 204
civility 223
civilization 251, 261
clairvoyance 16
clergy 16, 31, 72, 94, 170, 200, 222,
  315. *See also* religion
clubs (ladies') 21
communication 169, 175, 178
companions 215, 228, 359
competition 188, 218, 225
complexity 136
computers 122
conceit 300
conclusions 124, 319
conferences. *See* meetings, conventions
confidence 141, 222, 252
Confucius 275

conscience 246, 261
conscientiousness 93, 100
conservative 263
consistency 220
consumers, consumerism 98, 101, 102
controversy 140, 240, 309
convenience 176, 314
conventions 122, 243, 367
conversation 138, 141, 142, 144, 216,
  323. *See also* talkativeness
cooperation 203
corporations 95, 105, 118, 119, 200,
  204
courage 15, 202, 226, 240, 260, 298
courtesy 217
cowards 229, 326
creativity 146, 202, 320
credit (praise) 137
crime 160, 197, 198, 218, 230, 264
criticism 63, 133, 176, 257, 259
Cubans 264

Damocles 240
dancer 16
Danes 321, 332
danger 230
darkness 218
deafness 285
death 82, 139, 162, 179, 213, 214, 218,
  221, 226, 227, 230, 251, 254, 259,
  261, 285, 360
debts 119
decency 242
defeat 60, 263
democracy 256, 266
Democrats 243, 260
deviation 291
dictators 255, 256
dieting 125, 142
differences 133, 249, 270
diplomacy 134
direction 85, 313
disasters 162
discretion 219
disease 194, 248
dissent 70. *See also* differences
doctors 62, 294, 325. *See also* surgeons
  and "Doctors, Lawyers, Industry
  Chiefs," 185–195
doubters 115, 325
dreamers 239, 329
dreams 285

idealism 134, 267
ideas 76, 95, 103, 136, 137, 169, 251, 268, 312
ignorance 63, 145, 218, 224, 227, 293
imagination 147
imitation 288
impertinence 288
impromptu talks 15
improvement 140, 221, 222
income 118
India 276
Indians 331
inheritance 71, 82
innovation 312
inspiration 245
interference 19
introductions 14, 17, 24, 30, 243
Italians 196, 198

Japanese 118
Jesus 34
judgment 221, 224
justice (also, injustice) 196, 198, 252, 256, 260

kindness 282, 292
Kipling, Rudyard 324
knowledge (learning) 71, 74, 75, 80, 123, 137, 138, 173, 216, 218, 220, 222, 223, 224, 227, 228, 241, 253, 255, 285, 292, 293, 300, 301, 316, 324

lateness 201, 364
laughter 146
law, laws 196, 198, 241, 293, 300
lawyers 62, 261
leadership 216, 240, 242, 253, 254
learning. See knowledge
leisure 284, 314
liar 219, 289
liberal 263
liberty 241, 242, 249. See also freedom
lies 139, 219, 260, 264, 286
life, meaning of 141, 246, 250, 281, 317, 320
Lincoln, Abraham 125
lions 22
listening 316, 318
loafing 141
logic 162

longevity 159
love 310
loyalty 280
luck 147, 221, 297

madness 240
malnutrition 116, 142
Mao Tse-tung 300
marketing. See selling
marriage 143, 148, 160, 179, 196, 199, 200, 308. See also sex
meat-eaters 118
medicine 294
mediocrity 95, 287
meetings 97, 103
memories 221
mercy 191, 293
mergers 105, 204
microphones 18
military 98, 136, 201, 244, 265
mind 296
miracles 156
miserliness 32
misery 282
mistakes 134, 218
modesty 257, 260, 300, 324, 326. See also egotism
money 58, 135, 136, 190, 193, 202, 221, 223, 227, 244, 282, 283, 288, 289, 293
moon 251, 311
morality 291
morals 357
morning (early) 17, 201
mules 23

necessity 259
neighborhood 297
neighbors 196
new 298
news 219, 224, 313
Nixon, Richard M. 114, 115, 367
Noah (of Ark fame) 25
nobility 223, 284
nonsequiturs 190, 268, 319

obsolescence 121
old 298
opinion 146, 259, 328
opportunity 140, 218, 226, 317
originality 29, 33, 321
outer space 120, 251, 265, 311, 322

souls 161
Spanish 197
specialization 321, 327
speculation 126
speech 285, 297, 298
speech, freedom of 34, 143, 149, 188, 266, 267, 328
speed 121, 219
speeding 364
spirit 290
sports 146, 161, 314
starting 17
statistics 113, 125
status quo 137
stealing 197, 300
Stevenson, Adlai E. 24, 28, 59
strength 216, 226, 245, 267
stubbornness 148, 214, 220
stupidity 140, 146
suburbia 123, 139, 145, 204. *See also* housing
success 82, 96, 146, 147, 199, 200, 203, 214, 222, 262, 300
suffering 289
superiority 180, 250
supermarkets 117
surgeons, surgery 190, 194, 204. *See also* doctors
suspicion 230, 293
sweat 257

tact 326
talent 136
talk 287
talkativeness 96, 215, 216, 220, 222, 225, 231, 260, 280, 285, 287, 305, 308, 312, 318, 332
taxes 145
tears 257
technology 115, 120, 121, 122, 172, 250, 265
teenagers 70, 73, 74, 80. *See also* youth
telephones 103, 115, 121, 138
television 114, 115, 121, 169, 175, 176, 363
theory 30, 322
thief 197, 300
thirst 289
time 314

toastmasters 16, 21, 24
togetherness 103, 249, 258, 266, 270
toil 257
tongue 297
tradition 137
transportation 59
travel 121, 266
trust 147, 222, 284
truth 58, 59, 70, 137, 146, 149, 158, 173, 174, 216, 243, 258, 260, 282, 286, 289, 298
tyranny 241, 248, 252

understanding 146, 175, 300, 309, 331
United Nations 114
upper crust 362

vegetarians 118
venereal disease 122
vice 296
victory 252, 256, 258
violence 252
virtue 283, 296
vision 155, 225, 239, 241, 246, 251, 269
Von Braun, Wernher 311
voting, votes 61, 63, 244, 264

war 218, 240, 248, 253, 254, 255, 258, 270, 286
weakness 267
wealth 118, 119, 190, 224, 226, 230, 282, 283, 284, 288, 293, 324
Who's Who 21
willingness 217
winners (winning) 203, 229
wisdom 73, 76, 80, 104, 137, 156, 157, 159, 197, 219, 275, 282, 285
wisemen 19, 156, 157, 216, 220, 281
wit 223, 259, 280
women, women's lib 21, 29, 98, 145, 148, 199, 308, 364
words 138, 141, 222, 245, 255, 256, 263, 280, 281, 285, 287, 297, 298
work 93, 102, 145, 147, 149, 220, 224, 226, 228, 229, 246, 281, 283, 290
writers, writing 28, 32, 178, 190, 222, 256

youth 143, 157, 189, 191, 225